A Talking Dogs Book

www.scentwork.com

Published in the UK by Talking Dogs Publishing
49 Mayfield Road
Whittlesey
Peterborough PE7 2AY

© Pam Mackinnon 2013

The right of Pam Mackinnon to be identified as author of this work has been asserted by her in accordance with the Copyright Designs and Patents Act 1988

All rights reserved. No part of this publication may be reproduced, stored in a retrieval system or transmitted in any form, or by any means, without prior permission in writing of the author.

ISBN 978-0-9575897-0-4

Printed and bound in Great Britain

CONTENTS

PART 1

What is Talking Dogs Scentwork®?

Talking Dogs Scentwork® (TDS) is about teaching your dog to find a specific scent. It is a free flowing search style that allows the dog to cover complex areas efficiently and effectively. The handler works to support the dog and ensure the whole area has been cleared.

Talking Dogs Scentwork® would never have come into being were it not for a road trip conversation with my great friend Sue Sternberg. Her suggestion that I offer some scentwork training was the first time I'd ever considered using the skills I'd learned as a drug detector handler for HM Customs & Excise (as it was called) with my pet dog clients and colleagues.

I began by introducing occasional small searches as a part of my adult dog training classes. Much to my surprise, and delight, people really loved it. The dogs were animated and excited to work and owners were amazed at the scentwork skill their dogs displayed. I quickly realized that in order to allow everyone to participate, I would have to adapt some of the techniques to fit with dogs that had not been specially selected for their high drive, courage and willingness to work. By incorporating parts of other dog training disciplines, such as gundog work, and being flexible with the finds, using food as well as toys, I developed Talking Dogs Scentwork®.

Within the dog world there are a variety of search styles, each adapted to a specific task. Search and Rescue (SAR) primarily uses air scenting in order to cover large areas. It would be ridiculous to ask the dog to sniff every blade of grass in order to find someone lost on a mountain. Instead he must cast around to quickly find a scent he can latch on to, and off he goes with the handler following on. Working Trials search squares ask the dog to search alone for random items incongruous to the area rather than by a particular scent. So he might be asked to find a wooden or metal item in a grassy area. Obedience scent discrimination always asks the dog to identify one specific scent on a cloth from a pattern of unscented cloths laid out on the floor. The dog doesn't have to search the area to find the cloth, he has to work over the cloths that are clearly presented without any help from his handler. Tracking requires the dog to pinpoint a specific scent and lead the handler to the end of the trail. These dogs will use a combination of air scenting and ground scenting. Once they hit the scent trail they follow it until they find the person or article without much guidance or help from the handler. The handler is attached by a harness and long line so will be way back, relying on the dog to find the right scent and lead them to the article. Operational detector dogs are required to find a variety of learned scents in a variety of areas, indoors and out, at various heights and in various conditions working as a team with their handler. Each working style will suit particular dogs and they will be selected on the basis of the work required. Talking Dogs Scentwork® uses all these methods, allowing the dog to learn new strategies, build on favoured ones and to work together with his handler to reach the goal. This is why Talking Dogs Scentwork® is suitable for all dogs. The team work, used only by the detector dog teams, is what helps make this such a fun activity for both dog *and* handler.

Who can do it?

This style of scentwork can be used by everyone as the searches can be adapted to the skills, experience and ability of both the handler and the dog. Some people love to watch their dogs searching without any help from them. They hide something then send their dog into the area to find it. Others want to be part of the search, supporting their dog to find the ever more challenging hides. By tailoring each search to the participants, everyone wins. So people or dogs with mobility issues can join in, dogs that do not like to play with toys can find food instead and folks with ambitions to work professionally can hone their skills.

During my time as a professional drug detector dog handler I worked English Springer Spaniels. These were speedy, brave and hard working dogs that wanted to search all day long. Many pet dogs do not have this drive, this intense motivation to work. From an operational point of view they would not be accepted as a detector dog. From a pet point of view the intense drive to be constantly busy can be undesirable and difficult to live with. Through working with pet dogs and their owners my understanding of scentwork had increased tenfold. Scentwork is not limited to specific breeds, ages, physical abilities or courage. Some of the loveliest searches I've witnessed have been from a Great Dane, a Jack Russell Terrier and a Whippet. Scentwork teaches owners to be sensitive to their dogs' body language and their state of mind. Subtle changes in tail position or speed of movement can be the first signs that the dog has found the scent. By careful observation of their dogs, owners learn to spot these signals and in turn learn to identify what their dogs are saying and feeling in day to day situations, not just when searching. Confidence plays a huge part in scentwork. By recognizing drops or rises in confidence owners can better help their dogs reach emotional equilibrium.

Dogs with physical limitations can successfully participate in Talking Dogs Scentwork®. I have worked dogs that are blind, or deaf, and dogs with chronic joint or back problems. We adapt the searches and the handling to accommodate any issues and to maximize the dog's abilities. And dogs with mental or emotional issues can participate too. Dogs that do not relish the company of other dogs can search to their hearts content without the worry of having to interact with another dog. Dogs that are nervous and whose anxiety has inhibited learning have successfully learned Talking Dogs Scentwork® and have been able to work in places where previously they could not. This activity builds confidence and can help dogs improve their emotional state both during and after scentworking.

So, who can do Talking Dogs Scentwork®? Everyone can. And everyone can benefit from it.

Benefits of Talking Dogs Scentwork®

Talking Dogs Scentwork® is mentally exhausting. You can positively tire your dog out in a very short time. Scentwork requires great concentration, which is why dogs get tired so quickly. With physical exercise, the more you do it, the fitter your dog gets, not the more tired. By combining physical health with mental effort you will get a tired dog. I often see clients who complain that their dog never settles, even after a long walk. But 20 minutes of scentwork and their dog will be snoring on the sofa, satisfied and happy. Think of a really rainy day. You've been out once and you and your dog are finally drying off. You think, 'Do we really have to go out there again?' No! You can do some scentwork instead of that second, soggy walk. And while I would rarely advocate scentwork instead of all physical exercise, for some dogs staying at home is their only or best option, working on the mental wellbeing is just as important as working on the physical. And is much more often neglected. How often do you walk your dog? Every day? Great. How often do you train him? A couple of times a week? What does he do with his brain the rest of the time? Sadly, boredom is a fact of life for the majority of pet dogs. Banish boredom with Talking Dogs Scentwork®.

This activity is also an excellent way to reconnect with your dog, especially if your relationship has gone through rocky times. It builds trust and can help speed up bonding with newly rescued dogs. And it helps build concentration in young or impulsive dogs. The beauty of scentwork is that each dog works to his or her own ability, as handlers, trainers and assistants constantly respond and fine tune the search according to what the individual dog needs. And of course, it's FUN! Dogs are allowed to be dogs and engage in an activity that owners can often find annoying or worrysome. Instead of battling against their natural desire to search, owners can harness and control the search.

Search techniques can provide great help both with daily training and with some behavioural issues. From improving recalls to learning to cope with traffic, scentwork is an adaptable, effective tool to add to your toolbox and to your dog's skill set.

Part 2

How does it work?

How the dog's nose works – a quick guide!

The dog inhales the air, and the scent particles carried within it, through his anterior nares (nostrils), which dilate as he breathes in. The scented air passes through the dog's nose, a bony nasal cavity divided into two chambers by the septum, and is warmed and moistened through the turbinates, two spongy bones that are rolled into a cone shape and sit either side of the septum. It hits a small patch of tissue in the back of the nasal cavity called the olfactory epithelium, which is 30 times bigger in dogs than in humans. The olfactory receptor (OR) cells, neurons, (twice as many in dogs as in humans) in the olfactory epithelium act as sensory signaling cells due to the cilia, cellular antennae, on their surface which are in direct contact with the air. This causes a chemical stimulus that initiates an electrical signal firing neurons along the olfactory nerve to the olfactory bulb. The olfactory bulb is the part of the central nervous system through which the signal gets carried to the brain, specifically to the limbic system where interpretation of the smell begins. It has been estimated that as much as a third of the dog's brain is dedicated to scenting.

How scent works

Your dog's sense of smell is truly astounding. We still don't know for sure how much greater it is than humans, but it is thought to be between 10,000 – 100,000 times greater. The olfactory cortex, which works out what the scent is and it's relevance, in dogs is thought to be 40 times greater than that in humans. Everything has a scent and where that scent goes is often not obvious to us non-canines. To help clarify what your dog is working with, let's look at the three main elements of how scent works:

1. **The scent picture**
2. **The search item**
3. **The scent itself**

1. The Scent Picture

First of all, the plume or movement of scent is known as the scent picture. This picture can only be seen by the dog, not by the handler. While it is thought that scent can exist in a vacuum, it needs movement to create a scent picture or trail. The means of this movement is usually air. Where there is air and air flow, there will be scent. For example, wind or breeze will carry scent, as will the air all around us. Temperature is an extremely important element when looking at scent. Hot environments distribute scent making it large and fluid, whereas cold environments hold scents, making them small and more static. Think of the gutsy smells that come out of busy kitchens compared to the minimal odour of a cold store. The heat of the kitchen speeds up the movement of the scent particles causing the air to rise and so brings out the scent and distributes it freely around the room. People moving around in the kitchen will also disturb the air causing more distribution. This means that the dog is more likely to hit the scent early into the search, but might take longer to track it back to source. But in the cold store, empty of people, the scent particles will move slowly. The cold air sinks so it will take much longer and be more difficult for it to move away from the source. This will require the dog to do a more detailed search to pick up the initial scent but as it will be closer to the source, he should track it back faster. So both areas could take the same length of time to search and clear despite their very different conditions.

The scent picture will be affected if the hide is near a heater or a window or if it is outdoors or indoors, if the weather is hot or cold, windy or still. Temperature and movement of air is what the handler should be aware of - the dog certainly will be.   One of the best times to get a glimpse into this invisible world is when the dog is air scenting. His nose follows the trail of scent giving us a brief insight into how the scent is moving through the air.

The Kinetic Theory of Gases tells us that the particles move in a straight line until they collide with something. Depending on what they collide with, the scent will be distributed in a variety of ways but it will get weaker the further it travels from the scent source. As gases have many of the same properties as liquids, it may be easier to think about how water responds when it collides with solid objects.

When the sea moves over small objects such as rocks or pebbles, the water simply flows over and under them. So will air. Smooth objects allow the air to travel neatly over them without much disturbance. But hard edges tend to make small splashes up and out as the water or air moves over the top and on it's way.

Smooth, forward air travel over smooth objects

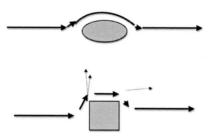

Sharp edges can cause the air to distribute up and out as it travels over the object

Consider where the sea goes when it hits cliffs. It goes up. It can't go over the cliffs so it hits against them, goes up and out a little, then drops. Water is heavier than air so it drops faster. But air will behave the same way when it hits a wall, moving up, out and down.

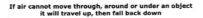
If air cannot move through, around or under an object it will travel up, then fall back down

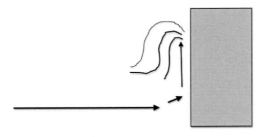

Next, consider what happens when the sea hits the promenade. It moves up the wall and then moves over the top continuing on in it's original direction. So air hitting a low cabinet will move up, over and on. Of course, if there are cracks in the promenade, some of the water will also continue straight on, moving into the cracks, just as air will if there is any space for it to move under the cabinet. This is not an either or situation, it can move in multiple places at once.

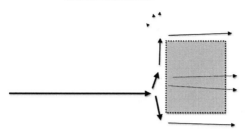

To figure out the likely direction of air flow, you have to look for objects that will affect the passage of the air, such as walls, trees, and furniture, and the sources of air flow, such as open doors and windows, vents, fans and people moving around. Just as water will soak into certain materials while it will pass over others, air does the same. Cloth, wood, plaster will all soak up some scent as it is carried in the area, while brick, metal or concrete retain very little but this may change depending on the temperature of those materials. When working indoors the height of the ceiling will affect the temperature and the air movement as will the ambient temperature of the room.

Imagine a scented article (see diagram) hidden in an open cardboard box in the middle of a room. Without any influence from air flow the scent would diffuse out of the box evenly in all directions. But there will be air flow. It's impossible for there not to be during scentwork as you and the dog will be causing air to move never mind any other factors. The dog's wagging tail alone causes quite a bit of turbulence in the air. Opening the door towards you and closing it behind you when you entered

19

the room will have pulled the air out and then pushed it back in. The fan heater pumping out hot air to the right of the hide will be pushing hot air towards the hide which will cause some of the scent to travel up towards the ceiling, while some of it moves towards the heat of the heater itself. The open window to the left of the hide will be letting cold air in which will cause the scent to fall but will also provide an opening for it to move through so some will go up and out. However, more of the air gets cold so moves down. The wooden floor will absorb more scent than the brick walls, and the high vaulted ceiling may hold the warm air as it rises and hits the cold air in the ceiling space. Can you see how complicated this is? But the dog can work this out very quickly, pinpointing the area with the strongest scent, which I would suggest may be up and to the right of the hide, and then working it back to the source. This is why we leave the scenting to the dog with the handler taking the supporting role.

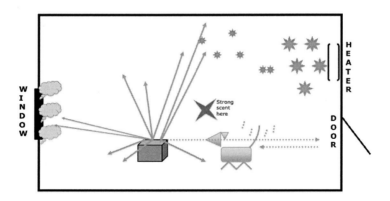

When working outdoors, the main factor will be the weather. I've talked about the effect of heat and cold, but what about rain, wind, frost or snow? Scent generally rises to the top of water. Static or stagnant water allows scent to rise, but rain is constantly moving so quickly washes scent away. Scent can float on streams but as the stream is flowing it doesn't remain for long. Frost and snow cool the air and make the scent move slowly. But it does hold the scent stopping it from dissipating too quickly giving the dog a good chance of hitting it if he gets close enough. Scent can sit on top of snow nicely allowing the dog to find it with ease. Scent underneath snow is a much trickier affair to locate. It can be done, but only if his nose and nasal passages aren't too cold and dry to stop them working effectively. Dogs need to have frequent access to water before, after and sometimes during, a search in order to keep them hydrated and keep the nose and nasal passages lubricated.

Wind is probably the most interesting and challenging weather condition to work with. It takes the scents to all sorts of unimagined places, it lets the dog hit the scent then carries it away again, it moves fast and far, very difficult. So dogs working in cold, stormy weather have the toughest job. Worth thinking about when you next see a SAR team, those folks are amazing.

As a brief rule of thumb, here are the main points to consider:

1. Temperature
2. Working indoors or outdoors on hot days, scent will generally rise when it hits a wall or solid vertical surface
3. Working indoors, scent will move around windows, doors and heaters, fans and air conditioners when switched on
4. Scent will soak into soft materials as it passes over or through them
5. Scent will continue to move past shiny, hard materials as it passes over them

6. Scent tends to pool in the corners of rooms as it has limited access to other areas (keeps bouncing off the two walls and or ceiling/floor)
7. Damp, or wet areas can often hold strong scent for short periods
8. When outdoors work your dog into the wind to give him the best chance of picking up the scent
9. Prevent people from walking around your search area as this will disturb the scent picture – unless you are doing it specifically to increase the challenge of the search
10. Make all things equal in the search area if possible, i.e. if you move one curtain, move them all, or one box, move them all, etc.

All of these factors must be considered when supporting the dog to find the source of the scent. Remember, only the dog can see the scent picture, so follow his lead. Trust your dog!

2. The Search Item

Secondly, the search item itself also has a scent picture. Porous, softer materials soak up and release scent more easily than impermeable, hard materials. So finding a metal object is likely to be more difficult than finding a toweling one. The amount of scent given out by the item increases as the item increases in volume, i.e. the bigger the item the greater the scent and vice versa. Using soft scented items in the initial stages of scentwork allows the dog to release more scent when playing with the item at the end of the search. Biting down on the article puffs scent out and so the relevance of scent is reinforced by the enjoyment of the game. You can use soft toys, such as the small mice we use in workshops which are about 6cm long. Or for bigger dogs fleece tug toys are an excellent vehicle for holding scent and providing a great game at the end of the search. Try to use the squashiest, smallest toy you can as very long, chunky or large toys can be limiting when it comes to finding good hiding places for them. Just ensure that they are not so small that your dog would swallow them, safety is paramount. Toys covered in tennis ball material are also good as the felt soaks up the scent nicely. Just remember whatever article you choose, the dog is learning to search for the scent on the article, not the article itself. This means that as he becomes more experienced you could put out a mouse, a tuggy and a tennis ball, but only one of them are scented. Or you could put out two unscented tennis balls and a new article that is scented. Furry pencil cases make great scent toys. They can be scented up as normal, or if you need to scent something quickly, you can pop some of the scent inside the pencil case and off you go. These little changes help to ensure that the dog is really searching for the scent and not assuming it will always be on the same article.

As the dog becomes even more experienced, the scented article can change to harder substances such a plastic, wood and rubber. These soak up and release less scent and so make for more challenging searches. Eventually, your dog can look for the scent alone, just smeared onto a surface in the search area. This provides the ultimate challenge.

3. The Scent

The final part of this aromatic trio is the scent itself. If we can smell it, the dog certainly can. If we cannot smell it, the dog probably can. I start dogs off on dried cat-nip, a distinctive, strong smelling herb that isn't available to most dogs on a daily basis. It may sound obvious, but you must not choose scents that dogs find unpleasant as these will deter the dog from searching. Dogs often dislike citrus or bitter smells. I have found that many dogs do not like the smell of aniseed, despite it being a popular scent in K9 Nose Work® trials in the USA. Due to the vomeronasal or Jacobson's organ, dogs can taste what they smell. So when choosing your scent allow the dog to give it a sniff. If he recoils or backs away, don't use it. If there is mild interest or no reaction, do use it. One colleague chose ginger as her dog's scent. This was an excellent choice as she was able to start with a food reward (a form of ginger cake) and then change over to ginger scented articles. Scents used in scent work trials in the USA are often oil based (this is a good carrier that releases scent easily) but oil or liquid based scents have some practical problems. The first and most important issue is that of safety. A great many substances and oils are toxic to dogs, including anise, peppermint and thyme. Of course, the dog should never be able to ingest the scent or oils during scentwork and the amounts they do accidentally ingest would be very small and are even found in many dog foods and treats in very diluted forms. But I always prefer to work on the side of caution so I recommend that you research to check if the substance you would like to use is safe for your dog so that you are fully aware of how much care you need to take. In addition to this it is very easy to use too much oil and so make the scent extremely strong. This can flood the scent receptors and actually make it more difficult for the dog to find the source. The strong scent will also cause a greater distribution of the scent particles and so contamination of anything it touches or comes close to can be a big issue. For example, if you hide an extremely heavily scented, oil based article in your living room behind the sofa, it will contaminate the whole sofa, and perhaps even the whole room, very quickly thus making it very challenging to conduct future searches in that area. Liquid based scents such as oil or liquid catnip soak into everything close by, both through smell and through physical contact. When these components meet material, you have very rapid contamination. However a dry, non-oil based scent, such as dried catnip or sage, will not cause the same level of contamination.

The other practical issue is that of storage. You need to keep your scented articles in an airtight container, preferably made of tin or glass as neither of these will let the scent seep out. Plastic containers can be used, but the longer they are used the more contaminated they will become and eventually the scent will leach through and out of them contaminating the cupboard, closet or cubby hole where it is stored. Tin is the most practical as it is light and portable. But oil or liquid will corrode the tin before too long. Corrosion causes rust and rust has a scent. Therefore, your dog may start searching for traces of rust as well as the scent you intended him to search for. All other scents that come into contact with the scented article will contaminate it, so by minimizing cross over in both directions, i.e. from scented article and to the scented article, contamination and confusion is minimized. If you wanted to teach your dog to find more than one scent, reliability increases if you use separate articles with each particular scent. This ensures that your dog is detecting each specific scent rather than only the strongest scent. And that he is not learning that all scents you want him to find have a common component, i.e. he can always smell the same strong scent no matter which one you actually think he is searching for due to mixing of scents on the same article Then, when you use a new toy that only contains the new scent, the dog may not indicate as he cannot detect the original, strong scent and so your training programme is flawed. Keep scented toys separate from each other in air sealed containers such as airtight food boxes. Having said that, I do not recommend teaching the dog to find multiple scents. It doesn't necessarily increase the fun of scenting and it brings with it many practical problems of avoiding cross contamination. Instead, searches can be made more challenging by reducing the strength of the scent or the size of the scent picture, lengthening the searches and varying height and location of hides. More on this later.

Bear in mind the safety of the toys and scents you use as your dog can, and probably will, come into contact with both the toy and the scent especially when you conduct proactive free searches with active indications. You can add Velcro® or press stud fastenings to favourite scentwork soft toys to make it easy to insert the scent should you want to use the toy quickly, e.g. you didn't have a toy 'cooking' in the scent tin. You can buy cat toys that have Velcro® sealed pockets that are ideal for this very purpose.

How to scent up an article

Sprinkle some catnip (or other scent) onto the bottom of your storage tin. The amount you use depends on the size of the tin. For example a Quality Street tin would take a couple of tablespoons, whereas an official TDS tin would take a couple of teaspoons. Place a piece of kitchen roll over the top of the catnip (this simply prevents mess when you use the mouse, you don't want to spread pieces of dried catnip around.) Then sit your unscented material article, be it a mouse or pencil case, tuggy or tennis ball, on top of that. Close the lid of the storage tin and leave for 24 hours. If you want to scent the article faster, use more catnip, perhaps wrapping some in a piece of kitchen roll and sitting that on top of the articles in the tin so that the scent is coming from above and below. Leaving the tin on a sunny windowsill or warm area will also bring out the scent more as the heat will help the scent become stronger and so be absorbed faster. After a day, your material article will be scented with catnip and ready to use for scentwork searches. Using something like catnip allows you to smell it too. Some people can't, but most can. Remember the rule, if you can smell it, you dog can definitely smell it, if you can't, he probably can. To start with scentwork, you need to take any doubt away that the article is scented. So if you can smell it, perfect. If you're not sure that you've left the article in the tin for long enough, leave it longer. Asking the dog to find something by scent means that you have to make doubly sure that the article does smell of the chosen scent. I recommend that you scent up several articles so that you always have one ready to use. This initial sprinkling of catnip should last for about a couple of months or so. After that time, empty the storage tin of the used catnip. Sprinkle in some fresh catnip as before and off you go again.

Some people like to use their own scent on the article. This is the scent that is used in obedience competitions on the scent cloths. However, I do not recommend using the handler's scent for Talking Dogs Scentwork®. To start with, everything in your house, your car, all your belongings, the dog's belongings, toys, etc. will carry your scent. In other words, you have contaminated everything you come into contact with. This contamination will be at a low level for some things, such as wooden furniture or unread books sitting on the shelf. Other things will be highly scented such as your bedding, or favourite chair. Working the dog in such a contaminated area as your home makes it much more difficult for him to find the actual article as not only will he have to identify the scent, he will also have to discriminate between the strength of the scents. He has to figure out that your favourite chair is not the article, but that the human scented mouse behind the chair is. Interestingly, when you go to other areas to search, ones that are not already contaminated by your scent, the opposite issue occurs. Your scent is not strong enough for the novice dog to detect. Unless the dog is searching a finite number of scent cloths, one of which he knows will definitely hold your scent, this scent is too weak, to difficult for him to find. Of course, once he becomes an experienced scentworker, he will be able to detect it easily, but at the initial stages of scentwork he needs a strong scent to help build his skills and confidence. When I worked Customs dogs they were trained to find four scents: cannabis, amphetamines, cocaine and heroin. The training always started with cannabis as it had the strongest scent. As the dogs learned to work additional weaker scents, such as heroin, were introduced. You need to give the dog the best chance of success, so don't use your own scent, use something new and distinctive.

Once you have used the article in a search, do not return it to the storage tin. I recommend putting it in a ziplock bag or container until you can wash it. Putting it back in the tin when it is used and soggy will contaminate the tin with the smell of your dog's slobber and make the dried catnip damp which in turn will make it rot and lose it's smell. Do not store the used articles in an area that you may want your dog to search as it will become contaminated with the used articles. I put mine on the kitchen windowsill where my dogs cannot reach it and it is a room that I never ask them to search. Wash the article at 60 degrees to help minimize the smell of both the catnip and eliminate the slobber. Washing will not eliminate the scent of the catnip, etc., but it will get rid of any other contamination. Don't use heavily scented washing powder as this will make the article smell of the washing powder scent which could confuse the dog. Which scent is he looking for, the catnip or the washing powder? Scent free powder for sensitive skins or just a tiny amount of your regular powder should do the job. It has been suggested that washing at a high temperature without using washing powder would clean and de-scent the article but as my washing machine takes an age to wash at high temperatures I haven't tried it. You could boil wash it in a basin, that would do the job. Once the article is dry, re-scent it as you did before. If you decide to teach multiple scents (though there is no real benefit to doing so), make sure to only use each article with one particular scent, don't mix and match between scents in order to prevent any cross contamination.

Part 3

Scentwork Skills

Handling skills

One of the joys of scentwork is that the dog must take the lead. The handler is there to support the dog and ensure the search is efficient and thorough, but must at all times work to the dog's agenda. Our movements are always guided by him. Even when we know where the hide is, we cannot know where the scent picture starts or ends. If we try to call the dog away from the scent picture and over to the hide, we will reduce his need to search. If we are going to tell him where it is, why would he bother to sniff it out?! More importantly, calling him away from scent will confuse him and may dent his confidence. If he's not indicating where we *think* he should be indicating and we move him away from the scent picture, he may become unsure of what we want him to do. I have seen strong, reliable dogs crumble within one search when called away from a scent. So we work with him, keeping enough distance between dog and handler that the handler can see what the dog is doing but not impede his progress. When he starts to indicate, give him space and support. Ask the question (more of which later.) Give him time to investigate. Stay back, don't crowd him. Let him make the decision about whether he's onto the scent or not. Get used to walking backwards so that you don't miss a thing. Working backwards means you won't be looking the other way when he indicates and are always ready to gesture to the next possible hiding place should he need your encouragement or assistance. In very hazardous areas, such as woodland, or during directed, linear searches like vehicles or people, walking backwards is not always necessary, or safe. But by then your dog should be working confidently and your eye for his indications should be well developed. By walking backwards during all initial searches, you get into the habit of always watching the dog. Quickly scan the area while doing your safety check before the search begins to identify any hazards, such as low beams, dips or bumps on the floor or furniture that you could bump into. Use your peripheral vision during the search to prevent you from tripping over or bumping into things which could distract the dog and hurt you. It is important that the handler moves lightly, quietly and swiftly. Clumping around the area will distract the dog. You need to match your pace to the dog's. If you move too slowly you will leave the dog waiting, looking for something to do. Inexperienced dogs generally do not carry on searching using their own initiative (this will come later), so if you are not ready to suggest an area or item to investigate, the flow of the search will be interrupted while the dog waits for you. This can lead to a drop in energy, which can then switch the dog off or produce frustration. If you go too fast and hurry the dog, he won't have time to search properly. So find the balance, wait for him to look up or towards you before you cue the next area. If you have a really speedy dog, do not worry. You won't have to run around if you position yourself well. Head for the middle of the search area so that you have easy access to all areas. As the dog becomes more experienced and the searches become more challenging, he will naturally slow a little.

Use a hand gesture to give the dog direction and suggests areas and items that might contain the hide. Your physical movement towards certain areas, strengthened by the hand gesture, is key to convincing the dog that he should work with you rather than on his own. He needs to know you can be of assistance. Assistance not control. The hand gesture should be fluid and fleeting. Using the whole arm rather than just the hand gives the dog a clearer signal. Simply pointing at areas to search is not clear enough and may encourage the dog to look just at your hand rather than in the direction you are suggesting. Specifically, the hand gesture should be that of showing a person to a seat, the hand opens, gestures towards the seat and then withdraws. Don't keep it stiff and inflexible like a shop dummy, move it with grace and purpose. But don't get to hung up on it, just make it natural, use it to show the dog the area, then move on to the next place.

When you are working the dog at heights or asking him to jump up onto things such as tables, chairs, wood piles, benches, etc. I recommend he wears a harness. There are many harnesses on the market. Go for a well fitted, comfortable and supportive harness that will allow you to hold the back in order to take the dog's weight as he jumps off things and be ready to support him as he jumps up onto things. The classic Karenswood Breast Harness is a good choice (this was the make used by RAF and Customs when I was handling) as it's simple and strong (see the resources page for more details). But my current harness of choice, and the one used by the Border Agency, is the Catac Working Dog Harness. It has a broad girth strap that will support the dog well. And is made of strong, but flexible webbing that will not stretch or snap, always a worry with leather harnesses. The harness should fit well and should not have raised handles or other protruding parts that could get caught during the search. It should not tighten or restrict the dog when pressure is applied, so no pull harnesses are definitely a no-no for scentwork. Go for wide webbing, quality materials and good fit. You are not using the harness to lift the dog, but to support him as he jumps up onto slippery or unsteady surfaces and to take the strain as he jumps down. Many Customs dogs were retired due to arthritis in the elbows and shoulders, a result of repeated unsupported landings. Get used to automatically putting your hand under the harness in readiness to take the strain, but without applying any pressure. Understandably, many dogs dislike being pulled or lifted by the harness so will stop working or pull away when the handler touches the harness. If you use a light touch that doesn't impede his progress, the dog will learn that you are there to support and help him, not control and restrict him. This means that you have to anticipate where the dog will move to next in order for you to position yourself well should you need to be close enough to physically support him or far enough away to give him space to work the area. Good handlers do this by subtly leading the search using search patterns and routines that both members of the team become accustomed to.

The method for moving the dog around the search area is surprisingly simple. You, the handler, simply move to wherever you want your dog to search. You don't have to say anything, call him over or even point. Quiet, swift movement around the search area will encourage your dog to move. By moving backwards, you remain engaged with the dog and so the teamwork will become strong. Play on the dog's curiosity. He will wonder why you've moved to a specific area so will move towards you to see if there's anything there. Using this technique you can cover the whole search area.

Always plan ahead, thinking about where to go next, ensuring that nothing is missed or repeated too often. Don't get sidelined or cornered. Don't stick in the same small area. Work from the inside of the area. That way you can access everything. If you find yourself on the outside you will get stuck, you will interrupt the flow and you will find it difficult to follow the search patterns. The upshot of that would be that things could get missed, the area would not be searched thoroughly.

To compliment the handling skills, you always have your voice. To start the search you need to think of a word or words that mean go find something using your nose. When I was in Customs, our search word was 'Fetch!' However, as most people use fetch to mean a seen retrieve, i.e. the dog is sent to bring back a toy he's just seen being thrown, it is more appropriate to use another cue to send the dog to search for an unseen item. I use 'Find it!' Other words you could choose include 'Seek', 'Search' or 'Scent'. It doesn't matter what cue you choose as long as it's not one you already use to mean something else. The cue is important as this lets the dog know that the scentwork game is on. It also lets him know when it is not. To make this extra clear for some dogs that so enjoy scentwork they want to do it all the time, you can put a specific harness or collar on the dog that is only used for scentwork games.

You give the 'Find it' cue at the start of the search, as you release or take your dog into the search area. You only need to repeat it when your dog asks for help. When he looks over to you or seems to be losing track of the task in hand, you can repeat it. Apart from that, you need to stay quiet, let the dog work. Don't witter on. Just watch, move and work with the dog. It's a dance, he is your partner.

Indications - How to tell if he's found something

There are two main responses that your dog can use to indicate he has found something: active and passive. **Active** indications are when the dog proactively tries to access the scented article. In many cases, this means the dog will go in and retrieve the article. This is particularly useful for helping identify the specific hide rather than a general area. A **passive** indication is a learned response, taught by the handler, when the dog stops and stares/sits when he hits a scent. In my day, all Customs dogs were proactive. They all tried to get to the scent showing me clearly where the drugs were stashed. My, very important, job as handler, was to ensure that my dog got as close as possible to the drugs but never came into contact with them. His safety was my prime concern at all times. I taught this by setting up searches where he could safely get to the article which contained the controlled substance we were searching for, and gleefully rip it out of the hiding place in order to play with it. The skill was in making training aids that were strong enough to withstand rough play, gave easy access for me to remove the drugs during the reward game but did not allow the dog to access the drugs at any stage. A skill that you will not have to learn as we will not be using anything that could pose a danger to your dog.

Currently, the Border Agency exclusively uses dogs taught to give a passive stare indication. Passive dogs started to come into Customs just before I left. They were used to search passengers. For example, I might be asked to search a plane with my proactive dog while my colleague searched the plane's passengers with her passive dog. Passive dogs allow handlers to search without coming into contact with whatever they are searching, e.g. people, and without touching the source of the scent, e.g. explosives. The detection of firearms and explosives was, and still is in many areas, the traditional use of passive dogs. For obvious reasons, it is not safe for the dog to dig at a land mine or retrieve a gun. But this style of searching has many more uses. People can be searched without being touched by dog or handler. They can be searched for multiple scents including money, food, drugs or weapons. Vehicles can be searched without fear of scratching paint. And air samples from many containers can be searched in seconds rather the hours it would take to search the actual containers. Hence the Border Agency and others can now use one dog to find a variety of scents, such as currency or drugs, in a variety of areas, whether on a person or in a postal sack.

There is a downside to passive indications. The trainer needs to be skilled in teaching a strong, reliable indication. And the handler needs to stay vigilant and maintain the training in order to prevent the dog from giving false indications. This is an issue because on indicating, the dog is instantly rewarded. So a smart dog will discover that when he sits he gets his reward. Therefore he may try sitting without actually finding the scent. I think back to housetraining a puppy. Every time the pup went near the back door I let him out, just in case he needed to toilet. Then there came a time when I had to determine if the pup needed to go to the toilet or did he just want to go outside to play? I made a judgment call. If I was wrong I found out fast, the puppy pee'd on the carpet. If I was right, he didn't. Operationally, the detector dog handler cannot make a judgment call. She needs to trust the dog implicitly. However, not finding drugs on a person does not mean the dog has given a false indication. He could have taken drugs that the dog can scent on his body. He might have been somewhere where other people were smoking drugs and so his clothes have taken on the scent. He may have carried drugs in his pocket a few weeks ago. Not finding drugs does not mean the dog has given a false indication. The only way to test that the dog is giving good, positive indications is through training searches and set up situations. When I was operational, whenever we heard of fellow Customs officers taking a domestic flight, we would give them a packet of a controlled substance to hide on their person or in their bags for us to find with the dogs when they touched down at the airport. Training had to be this rigorous and real to ensure that our dogs were doing the best possible job. Without continuous training and testing, false indications can quickly creep into the dog's repertoire. This issue is more prevalent in passive than active dogs because the passive dog receives an external reward provided by the handler, whereas the active dog's reward comes directly from the article which he can access himself.

You will start to recognize how your own dog's body language changes when he hits or detects the scent. You will already be aware of changes in your dog's behaviour and demeanour when he hits certain scents. For example, you will recognize when he is sniffing where another dog has urinated. Or when he is about to drop his shoulder and roll in something smelly and disgusting (to us, not to him!) Or when he lifts his head and is about to run off after a deer or jump up onto the table to help himself to your roast dinner. I was able to spot the difference in my detector dog when searching butcher's baggage or even a certain type of aftershave. My dog's indication would be slightly different to his usual one. I would flag up the bag to my colleagues who would then search it to confirm my suspicions. Of course, had there been drugs in there too, my dog would have given his usual drug indications. Hiding contraband or controlled substances in food is a common tactic used by criminals. But this is a great way to help dogs find the smuggled item as anything that has a strong odour of it's own will carry the scent of the drugs, money, etc. out with it and so will actually aid the dog in detecting the scent.

Common changes in behaviour that indicate the dog has found the scent include:

a) **the check step** - the dog suddenly goes back to double check an area or item he has just passed
b) **dog closes his mouth** – closing the mouth allows the dog to use his nose more effectively, ensuring that all the scent hits the very best scent receptors in his nose rather than his mouth
c) **dog changes speed** – some dogs, such as spaniels, speed up and work faster; others, such

as Rottweilers, slow down as they recognise the scent

d) **tail position changes** – the tail can become vertical, can drop, wag very quickly or slow right down

e) **dog becomes more intense** – the body becomes less flexible, more rigid, the focus becomes more noticeable as the dog fixes on an area

f) **further investigation** – the dog lingers at the same spot as if checking it more thoroughly than other spots he has already passed, quite often he will move on to another area but return to this area as if comparing them in order to narrow the scent picture and pinpoint the find

g) **'Bisto' kid** – the dog starts air-scenting, as if he's following an invisible trail in the air, just like the kids in the old '*Ahh, Bisto*' adverts.

Dogs will show all of these indications and a whole lot more. Observe them carefully, learn what they mean. These are the clues the dog is picking up in order to solve the puzzle you've set him. When you first start scentwork with your dog, it can be difficult to see these sometimes subtle signals. The answer is to video the searches and then watch them back at your leisure so that you have time to rewind, repeat and review the recording.

How to respond to an indication

When you see changes in your dog's behaviour, ask him 'Have you found something?' or 'Where is it?' This is an acknowledgement to the dog that you have noticed a change and gives him support and encouragement to investigate the scent picture. It may be that on further investigation he finds nothing there and moves on. That is fine, he can 'see' the picture, you can't. Even if you know the item is right there, remember that the scent may be flowing from another direction. If you ask the question and the dog becomes more intense, more excited, then continue to encourage him to work his towards the find. 'Where is it?', 'Have you got something?', 'What you got then?' are all examples of how to keep him working, keep him following the scent in order to lead you directly to the source. When you ask the question, you must allow the dog to answer yes or no. As you ask the question, step away from the dog. This can very difficult at first because you will be as keen as the dog to see if he got it right. It seems counter intuitive to step away instead of towards the dog. But if you step towards the dog, he may take that as a signal that you know where the hide is, that you are stepping towards it. In turn, the dog can become more excited and you can mistake this as further or stronger indications, which in turn make you move closer. Ultimately you can both convince each other that you know where the hide is and so end up disappointed and confused when the article is not where you expect it to be. So, ask the question and step away. Interestingly, stepping away is unlikely to draw the dog away from the scent picture. If he's hit the scent, he will want to stay with it. Walking backwards helps greatly with this because you can move away from the dog while remaining engaged with him. If he has not found the scent and the answer to your question is 'No', then he will move away with you. When that happens, use the hand gesture to suggest somewhere else to search and continue on. Asking the question should not be used as a diagnostic tool to figure out if the dog is actually indicating. It is there to prompt the dog to work towards the scent source or to move on to work in another part of the search area. Feel free to ask the question several times during the search, but only when you think you are seeing indications.

Once you know he has hit the scent, encourage him to work right to the source. Stand back, give him the space to work it out. If you move in too fast he will stand back to let you look for it. Nothing builds confidence like the dog locating and retrieving the find himself. You are there to give support, and to provide assistance should he really need it, but his job is not complete until he pinpoints the article. If he needs to push something out of the way, rip something, find a direct route or stand on something to access the hide you can start the drive in, an escalating commentary that encourages the dog to go for it. 'Go on then. You find it. You get it. Good lad. Well done. Good boy.' Your tone starts as a questioning one, and then gradually escalates in excitement and encouragement peaking when he pinpoints the item. You should be ready to pull back with the drive in or maintain it for a longer period at a steady but always encouraging tone. I have had to drive a dog in for minutes at a time. Doesn't sound long, but give it a try (without your dog) – it can be tricky. You don't want to peak too soon, turn the drive in into a nag or a distraction. You have to pitch it just right. But when you do, it can be a valuable asset.

Hiding the article

Hiding the article is a skill in itself. It always has to be appropriate to the dog doing the search. Sometimes, it has to be appropriate to the handler when you are working on your own handling skills rather than the dog's searching ability. For example, when the handler is having trouble seeing the indications and having time to react to them, a longer search with a deeper hide can be very useful. By setting up a search where the article is hidden inside several boxes but is emitting a good, strong odor, such as a soft toy saturated with the scent of cat nip, the handler can have a bigger indication to spot and more time to practise the questions and commentary leading to the scent source before the dog actually retrieves the article.

Do not try to place the article then discover it won't fit / stay in position. Ascertain these factors **before** you place it to avoid contaminating the hide. Use your right hand to test the space, see if the article will fit, while holding the scented article in your left hand. As your right hand is used to guide the dog and suggest places to look, this is the one that should always remain uncontaminated by the scent. You can make articles easier, or harder, to locate by disturbing the air flow around the hide. If you have a room full of boxes but only one box has been moved, the air flow around that one box will have been disturbed. This disturbance can be detected by the dog and so draw him towards that particular box. If you move several boxes you create several disturbances so not just one box is highlighted. This makes the search more difficult and the dog has to ensure he detects the scent within the disturbance rather than just the disturbance itself.

You can build on this by disturbing multiple objects in the area. You could move several boxes and shake a few curtains or move a few cushions, chairs, plant pots (depending on where you are working.) Obviously, as you disturb the areas, you must try not to contaminate them with the scent you want the dog to find, so use your feet or clean your hands if possible.

Some areas could be described as self-disturbing. These are areas where there are air flows caused by windows being open, heaters pumping out hot air, moving parts such as found in engine rooms, and any searches done outside. Weather plays havoc with scent pictures, diluting them, dispersing them and sending the scent in the opposite direction to the hide. This is the reason that outside searches are more difficult than indoor, where the environment is much more easily controlled. And hence why I prefer to start scentwork indoors, to set the dog up for success.

Once you have hidden the article, do not leave the storage tin or used articles either in the search area or close to it. The dog will find them and then have to be worked away from them adding extra time and effort to the search which it need not. It can cause confusion in early searches and use up valuable, limited time in later ones.

Practicalities

When using the same area to conduct multiple searches, make a note of where you have hidden the article. You need to know when the dog is indicating on a previous hide in the same area. You can then acknowledge the indication ('Good lad') and help the dog move on to continue the search. And this will help you keep track of where you are placing articles so that you are progressing on with the dog not just using the same or similar hides. For advanced dogs, placing a new find in a previous hide is a real test of the handler's skills in reading the dog.

Safety Check

Before starting any search, you should get into the habit of performing a safety check. This consists of your going around the area checking for hazards that could be dangerous to you or your dog. On an operation search, the dog handler would be the first, and only, person to go into the area to be searched. lots of people in the area, moving things around, cause great air disturbance and make it more difficult for the dog to search. The dog will still find whatever might be there, but it will take longer and so be less efficient. The handler must check for needles, glass, look for moving parts in machinery or pallets of boxes not safely stacked. Only once the handler is satisfied that the area is safe for the dog would she then begin the search.

Common hazards for pet dog owners to look out for include:

- ❖ Cables and flexes hanging down from computers, lamps, etc. You see these every day but are unlikely to really notice them.

- ❖ Electrical sockets – these would always be searched by operational dogs, but must not be searched by pet dogs. There is no reason to put your dog's wet nose anywhere near electrical sockets. As an additional measure turn the socket switches off.

- ❖ Hot areas such as radiators, fires, exhaust pipes, ovens, etc.

- ❖ Slippery surfaces, at ground level and on tables and higher surfaces. Also check for stability before asking your dog to jump onto something

- ❖ Toxic or hazardous substances such as bleach, petrol, cleaning products, oil commonly found in the kitchen, bathroom, sheds and garages.

- ❖ Sharp edges, rubbish, tin cans, etc.

- ❖ Broken glass on the ground or in or around cars

- ❖ Holes in the ground or loose rubble that you could slip on or the dog could get caught in

❖ Food, not so much of a hazard as a distraction, but worth removing before the search begins.

You must decide what to do about any hazards you identify. You can make them safe by laying them down, making them steady or removing them from the area.

Using cardboard boxes

Anyone who has been to my workshops will know that I use cardboard boxes as hides, especially in the early stages. This is for purely practical reasons. Most workshops are conducted in halls that contain very little bar chairs and a few tables. Therefore I need something to hide the article in. There is nothing particularly special about using boxes. I know that some methods of teaching pet dog secentwork place particular emphasis on boxes, but I do not. If you are reading this manual and want to start your dog searching at home, there is no need to clutter your house with cardboard boxes. You have lots of things already in place that you can use, such as tables, chairs, bookcases, beds, storage, rugs and much more. The boxes I use are the simply to use the space in the middle of the room and provide something that allows the dog to smell but not see the article. If you are running out of places to hide things, then of course you can use boxes, but I just wanted to highlight that they are not necessities.

When you are using boxes, perhaps at a training venue, you do need to consider the material/quality, size and previous contents of the box.

Material/Quality
Not all cardboard is equal. You will know this if you have flattened down boxes for recycling. Some squash in a

second, others you have to jump on to flatten. The difference is the thickness of the cardboard. Some very rigid boxes are made up of several layers of flat and/or corrugated cardboard. The thicker and more rigid the cardboard, the harder it is for the scent to pass through. The fibres of the cardboard are closer together and there are more layers for the air and scent to negotiate their way through. Whereas thin, cheap cardboard is the opposite and they will quickly become saturated with scent.

Additional layers of paper or card applied on top of the cardboard will also hinder scent movement. Many boxes have printed covers applied on top of the cardboard. The basic rule is that the glossier the outside of the box, the tougher it is for scent to pass through. So challenging boxes to hide articles in include very thick, rigid, glossy boxes that have contained computers or electrical appliances. Good starter boxes are plain, thin cardboard.

Size
The size of the chosen box must be defined by the size of the dog. The box is too high if the dog can't reach the article without tipping the box over or jumping into it. And it's too deep if the dog has to go all the way inside to retrieve the article. Avoid these issues in the initial stages of scentwork. They can be introduced as extra challenges in later searches. You want to set your dog up to be successful, to build confidence and have fun retrieving the article himself. If you have to help him retrieve it, he may come to rely on you to always get it for him rather than only when it is completely inaccessible.

A bigger box may also dilute the scent more as it travels around a larger area inside the box, but does create a bigger scent picture (assuming there is flow from inside to outside the box.) A small box allows for less dilution but creates a smaller scent picture. However, unless you are comparing a box that contained a fridge freezer with a matchbox, in most situations this makes little difference. But it's always good to know what the scent is likely to be doing in the hide.

Previous contents

Whatever was in the box, before you used it for scentwork, will have left a scent inside the box and in the cardboard. Scents can come from inside and outside the box, so it will smell of where it's been stored as well as what it contained. The smell of foodstuffs, both human and pet, can confuse the dog, drawing him over to the box that smells of food and away from the box that smells of catnip. In the later stages of scentwork this is fine, but it can cause dilemmas for the starter scentworker. So avoid using boxes that contained cereal, dog food, cat food, veterinary medicines (the outside is likely to smell of the veterinary practice and/or of animals) and boxes that have been stored in areas where mice or vermin could have contaminated them, such as sheds or garages.

The final consideration is how to use the boxes. You have so many choices. Let's split them into easier and more challenging configurations:

Easier

The box could be open and upright or open and on it's side. Facing towards the dogs as he enters the search area could be easier than facing away. Closing one flap of the box over is still pretty easy as it gives the dog good access to the scent but shields the article from sight.

You can tip the box up so that it balances on one edge on another box. Only do this if the dog won't be spooked by the box moving or falling off the other box. The box could be left open but the open end could be pushed up against another box to give a slightly more challenging search.

More challenging
All the flaps of the lid closed over. Boxes hidden inside other boxes. Boxes turned upside down, flaps open, so that the article is actually on the floor rather than touching the box at all. Placing the box with the article at he very edge or in the corner of a search area can be more of a challenge as they are easily missed during a search.

Cheese squashed into the corners of the box or under the lid flaps so that the box looks empty. Cheese in the corners with the box turned upside down is great as most dogs then hit the scent from the outside of the box. The fat of the cheese soaks into the cardboard and the corner allows air to escape so making this a nice hide. However, I've placed this in the more challenging section because even though the dog can smell the cheese it cannot access it without help unless he is particularly confident and creative in which case he'll flip the box over or chew through it!

Once you have used a cardboard box to hide food, it should not be used again as it is likely to have been contaminated by the dog (saliva) when he found the previous food article. Where there is little or no canine contamination on a box used to hide a non food article, it can be used again. However, if not being used immediately, it must not be stored with boxes that have been used.

Additional tips

1. You can use disposable rubber gloves when handling scented items. It is extremely easy to cross contaminate scents. This helps reduce that risk. You can also use tongs if you don't want to touch the item at all. However, dogs are extremely good at working despite mild contamination in the area so all is not lost if you forget.

2. Keep your hands clean so that when you are guiding the dog and holding the lead, they don't pick up the scent from either hand.

3. When practicing or working, remember where you hid the articles and, if scented, what scent they were. This helps explain why your dog may appear to give 'false' indications, i.e. he indicates that he has found something but there is nothing there. There may have been something there a few weeks ago that he can still smell. This lets you acknowledge his indication ('Good lad') and then move him one to continue searching the area.

4. If the weather or environment is hot, the dog will pant more. Panting and sniffing are mutually exclusive, so perform searches before hard exercise, or in the cool of the morning rather than the heat of the afternoon.

5. Give your dog a chance to rest between searches – this is fun but it is also hard work. Offer him a drink of water and put him into a settle, or back into the car or his cage.

6. As your dog hones his skills, you need to ask other people to hide the items. If you always know where the item is, you can miss indications, try to over-ride the dog and reduce the teamwork between you. When the handler does not know where the item is hidden, this is known as a blind search.

Part 4

The Search

Search Types

Free search

The free search is the first opportunity for your dog to scan the area to see if he can catch a whiff of the scented article. There are no restrictions on the dog when he is free searching, he can go high, low, anywhere he wants. Some dogs work very fast and will run around the search area. Others will wander around at a steady pace. But as long as both are sniffing, they are working. You will see dogs moving from one side of the area to the other, in a similar way to gundogs when they are quartering in a field. Both have the same aim, to pick up the scent and work it back the root.

During the free search, the handler's job is to keep a close eye on the dog, to keep out of his way and to subtly move him around the space if needs be. The easiest way to think about your movements is to imagine you are in a pinball game, bouncing off an invisible bubble around the dog that sends you in the opposite direction to him. If he moves to the left, you move to the right. If he goes North, you go South. This constant movement keeps the search energized and flowing. It encourages to the dog to cover the whole area. They will naturally move towards you so just by positioning yourself so that the whole search area is accessed you can ensure the dog will move into those areas too. In general if you work around 2m / 6ft away from the dog you will be close enough to observe and assist but far enough away to avoid hindering the search. You will be walking backwards while moving around, never taking your eye off the dog, always ready to ask the question 'Have you got something?', give encouragement as the dog gives something a good sniff and remind him to keep working should he look up or at you by saying 'Find it'.

The free search helps the dog become familiar with each particular search area. He can figure out what he can jump on or go under and where the boundaries are. It also gives him time to settle into the search before he has to do the more challenging patterns.

Directed search
Having completed the free search and the corners (see the section on search patterns) without locating the find, the next step is to start the **directed** search.

The directed search is a much more specific and thorough search. The purpose of this type of search is to help the dog examine the entire area in detail ensuring he checks high, low and everything in between. Unlike the free search where the dog can move back and forth between sections of the area, the directed search involves the dog and handler systematically working along the area together. An example would be working along a stretch of wall in the living room. This might include a skirting board, dado rail and radiator. So you would guide the dog up to the dado, down to the skirting board, behind and around the radiator. **As this is for fun, for reasons of safety I do not recommend searching electrical sockets.**

To start a directed search, place yourself directly in front of the dog, guiding with your right hand. If this search is done on lead, hold it in your left hand. Walk backwards along the search area using your body almost as a block to stop the dog going past you. Keep your body facing the dog and close to the thing you are searching. Leaving too much space between your right side and the area, such as the perimeter of a room, or item, such as a vehicle, provides the dog with the opportunity of rushing forward and past you. Ideally you want to move the dog forward (while remembering to walk backwards yourself) without having to go back and re-search the section. Backtracking interrupts the flow of the search and is inefficient. Constant interruptions can demotivate the dog and reduce his desire to work so closely with you. *However* – if the dog hits the scent and wants to move past you, step aside and allow him to go, hence why your body shouldn't actually block or prevent him from moving past you towards a scent. Make a mental note of where he broke off the directed search. If he indicates, ask the question 'Have you got something?', step back and get ready to help or drive him in to get the find. If he does not indicate or moves away from the area when the question is asked, bring him back round to the spot where he broke off the directed search and resume searching. In order to maintain the correct position, i.e. you walking backwards in a clockwise direction, always bring the dog round to the right so that you are between him and the perimeter. That way the search can flow on all the way around and nothing should be missed.

Working the dog on lead can help focus his attention on one specific area and prevents him from going too wide and covering areas not included in the search. The lead is used for times when it would be unsafe for him to work off lead, most especially vehicle searches. On lead searches are also used for searching people in order to keep the dog safe from them, and them safe from the dog should they be frightened or nervous of dogs. Working on lead also helps the handler learn to maintain body position, and see the indications closer up. This can be difficult as the dog is so close, but by asking the usual question 'Have you got something?' and moving away as normal, you can see more of the dog and so better interpret his actions. The lead should be long enough to allow you to do this. A standard length lead is fine, but a slightly longer one is better.

Blind search

This is when the handler does not know where the hide is. The handler is working blind, without knowledge of where the scented article has been hidden. The advantage of the blind search is that the handler must learn to identify the dog's indications. You must rely on the dog to tell you where it is as you have no other way of knowing. Make sure not to search for the article yourself when doing a blind search. Look for areas for your dog to search, not for you to find it.

My preference when first starting out with TDS is to have someone help so that you can have blind searches. This is the fast track to learning your dog's indications and trusting him. However, if you have chosen to teach your dog a passive indication, then I do not recommend blind searches until your dog's indication is strong and reliable. You don't want to risk cueing him at the wrong time, e.g. asking for the sit indication when he finds the article, rewarding if he indicates at the wrong place, e.g. he just sits anywhere rather than sitting because he's found the article, or confusing him in this difficult task. This means you have to be extra strict with yourself in not assuming you are seeing an indication because the dog is close to the hide. To help make sure this doesn't happen, video your searches. If you assume the dog has indicated when he has not, you may actually prevent the dog from giving good indications as you have been inadvertently telling him where the article is!

Known search

This is the opposite to the blind search. The handler knows where the hide is in a known search. You may have hidden the article yourself or have been told where it is by your helper. It is useful for passive searches (as discussed in the Blind search section.) Also for when you do not have a helper. Or when you want to practise in specific areas, introduce new elements or assist a dog more.

But handlers must treat known searches with caution and respect. They can encourage lazy handling, give inadvertent cues to the dog about the location of the hide and reduce your trust in the dog. So, use known searches sparingly and with care.

Blank search

During the early stages of scentwork, you will have very little time to practise your search patterns as the searches will have been designed to be quick and easy for your dog. As your dog's skills grow it can be difficult to grow your own handling skills. No matter how you try, the dog locates the find too quickly. You don't get a chance to practise your search patterns as he finds it on the free search. The answer to this is blank searches. Blank searches are where there is no pre-placed article. In other words, the dog searches an empty room and once the whole search is complete you can put out a quick, easy find as a reward for all his hard work. Now don't be thinking that this is tricking the dog (something I am very much against.) Everything is as normal to the dog, the search is the same, just longer and he still gets his find at the end. If you can get someone to trick you, the handler, that is ideal. If you search as though there is something there, the dog will too. But if you knowingly do a blank search, it can be all too easy to skip areas, not search as thoroughly safe in the knowledge that you've not missed the find. But you can learn to act through it so that you can eventually do blank searches wherever and whenever you and your dog like.

The blank search gives you time. Time to do the corners, the perimeter, the interior. It teaches you to be thorough. Did the dog really search the corner or did he just wander over there? Hiding finds in the corners will help both dog and hander ensure that they literally don't cut corners. But back to the blank search. Once the area has been cleared, i.e. you can confirm there was nothing to find, you can surreptitiously drop the article behind you, ideally just tossing it behind a chair or object close by. If you have an assistant they can place the article as you get near the end of the search, but they too need to be sneaky as they do it so as not to alert the dog to this twist in the game. The article doesn't want to be just lying in the middle of the floor, but as long as the dog has to do a quick search to find it, it's fine. Operationally, search dogs do not find contraband at each and every search. But they will find a reward or two every day by using this technique. Once the handler has declared the area clear, they will often get a colleague to hide the article for them. On other days when there is time to top up training they will use much more difficult hides, perhaps practicing on a concealment similar to one found by a fellow dog team or based on smuggling intelligence. The blank search is what allows the dog to build up their stamina and concentration required to search for the most challenging hides and taxing areas.

Blank searches also help the handler learn how to properly clear an area. With the initial searches, the search stops once the article is found. Now, searches can go on longer and so become more thorough. Having the confidence to say that there are no hidden articles in an area is an important skill. The handler has to be sure that they haven't missed anything, while still working efficiently and to the duration that is comfortable for the dog. Repeatedly searching the same area can be tiring, puzzling and frustrating for the dog. An interesting observation is that dogs do keep track of where they have searched and I have often witnessed dogs either coming to a complete stop or being reluctant to continue searching when asked to search the same area/item repeatedly. The dog knows it's clear, but the handler doesn't fully trust the dog. A practical way to address this issue of over-searching the same area, is to set a time limit on the search. That way, everything has to be searched efficiently and thoroughly the first time.

Search patterns

When you are searching with your dog it is very easy to forget where you've been, what you've already searched and what you've still to check. Even searching a room with six boxes scattered around, it can be difficult to keep track of which box has been searched. Consider trying to remember what you've searched in a large cargo shed with dozens of rows of shelving stacks or a multi-level engine room with storage areas and moving machinery. While you might not have access to such exciting areas with your pet dog, a village hall with stacked chairs, meeting rooms, cupboards and toilets can be just as complicated. To help search efficiently and save you having to remember what you have searched, there are a series of patterns to follow. By using the template of the various search patterns they should become second nature and so you will be better able to concentrate on your dog. This results in you being less likely to miss any indications and more likely to search the whole area.

Here are the patterns in the order that they should be done:

1. Free search
2. Corners (or zig-zags)
3. Perimeter
4. Interior

1. Free search

As previously described in the *Type of Search* section.

2. Corners

Once your dog has settled into the search and you feel that he's been over the whole area, you can move him into the corners. It is easy to literally cut corners when searching so this part of the search routine ensures nothing is missed. Pick a starting corner, whichever one you're nearest to, and as the free search ends, encourage the dog to 'Find it' by stepping to the right of the corner and gesturing in there with your right hand. This should send the dog to search in that corner. As he steps into the corner, you quietly and quickly step out and move diagonally to the second corner. By going to the corner diagonally opposite you give the dog another chance to scent through the middle of the search area. When he looks up from his first corner search, he sees you waiting at the second corner and heads over. You say 'Find it' and as he moves into the corner you move to the next one along. As before, once he's finished searching corner two he sees you at corner three and moves over. Finally, while he's searching this corner you move diagonally over to the final corner, which he can search when he's finished in corner three. You are still walking backwards as you move from corner to corner. If you turn your back to walk over to the next corner you would miss any indication the dog might give at the previous corner. By following this pattern, you will have searched all four corners and crossed through the middle of the search area twice.

Some areas are too large to follow the diagonal pattern. You couldn't physically move to each corner fast enough plus you'd be too far away from the dog to spot any indications or provide assistance, e.g. if he wanted to jump up onto something. In these situations substitute the diagonal pattern for a zig-zag. Starting at one corner, move diagonally across to the boundary of the area, then diagonally over the other opposite boundary. Keep doing this until you have zig-zagged your way along the whole area from end to end. This pattern does mean that you will miss two of the corners, but you will still cover the majority of space. The diagonal and zig-zag patterns are an extension of the free search. Those corners will be thoroughly searched at a later stage of the search.

As you are gesturing with the right hand and moving backwards, it can help you maintain your position if you start the zig-zag at the bottom left corner so that you can move to your right. As you come to the opposite boundary, turn right to face that boundary so that you are all set to back over to the other side. As long as you always turn to your right as you zig-zag along, you should be in the correct position. Later, as your handling skills become more fluid and automatic, you will be able to start from the nearest, most appropriate corner.

If the search area is an irregular shape or doesn't really have corners, just ensure that your perimeter search is very thorough.

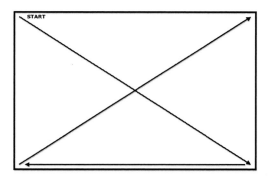

Corners pattern

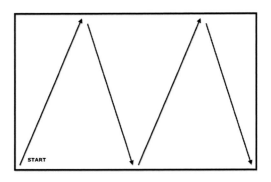

Zig zag pattern

3. Perimeter search

After you have finished the corners, you should start the perimeter search. This is a directed search, off lead. Wherever possible, always choose the same starting point. This saves you from having to remember a different one every time, a more difficult task than you would think. I always start at the door I entered to get into the search area. I then work clockwise around the perimeter of the room, walking backwards and using my right hand, which will be closest to the wall or boundary, to suggest where the dog should put his nose. The direction is important as you want to guide the dog, watch the dog and keep out of his way. Walk backwards, guide the dog with your right hand and keep moving around the outer edge of the area. By introducing the routine of always guiding the dog with your right hand you help him become an efficient searcher. And don't worry, you will get used to walking backwards while still watching where you are going. Keep the search flowing, try not to stop and start too much. You should always be moving to the next spot as your dog is working

When working with an inexperienced dog, always show him specific objects to search. Pointing at thin air, floors or walls gives him very little to focus on in these early stages and so he won't know how to deal with them. Instead, suggest furniture, pictures, boxes, etc. for him to search, moving quickly past 'dead' space. Once he becomes more experienced he will learn that things can be hidden under carpets, inside walls and on the ceiling.

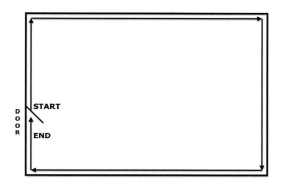

Perimeter pattern

4. Interior

If nothing has been found during the free, corner or perimeter searches, it's time to search the inside of the area. This can be more difficult to work in a set routine as it depends on how the area is laid out. For example a classroom with chairs and desks in rows provides a logical pattern, whereas a room filled with chairs and desks set out randomly does not. The basic rule of thumb is to start at the same point where you began the perimeter search, i.e. at the entrance to the search area. Working clockwise, search everything in your path around the area. In large areas you may end up working in a spiral, from the edges into the middle. Or working up and down in lines. In smaller areas you may be able to access everything in a logical pattern in just one circuit around the interior. Whichever pattern you choose, be logical and stick to it. Otherwise things will be missed.

When you are searching items in the interior of the area, such as boxes, furniture or machinery, if they are big enough that you need to walk around them to search them fully, you will need to work them in an anti-clockwise direction. The easiest way to remember which way to go is to always make sure that your right hand is closest to the thing you are searching, be it a wall, car, box or sofa.

Here's the simple rule:

If you are **inside** the thing you are searching, work **clockwise**.
If you are **outside** the thing you are searching, work **anticlockwise**.

So, you are inside a room, therefore you work clockwise. But you are outside the table, so work anticlockwise.

This may all seem rather complicated but once you get into the habit of working like this, you'll not even think about it, you'll just do it automatically.

At the end of the search where you have conducted a free search, done the corners and perimeters plus everything on the inside you will have found the article or declared the area clear (blank.) If the area is not blank but you've not found the article, check the troubleshooting section.

This thorough search using the search patterns is more tiring for the dog so start with small areas and gradually build up to searching for 10 – 15 mins.

Interior pattern

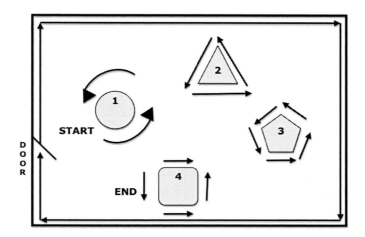

Manage the search area

With many larger or more challenging areas, the most efficient way to search them is to break them into smaller sections. Work the free search over the entire area. Then split the area into more manageable sections, following the remaining 3 search patterns in each individual section before moving to the next section. The less you have to remember the less chance there is of missing something or re-searching the same area. By splitting the entire search area into two, three or more manageable areas, the search is simplified.

Part 5

Getting Started

Getting started

I suggest that you select either an active or passive response for each scent you choose. Overall, it is easier for the dog to always give the same response to every scent. If you do choose to teach one response to one scent and a different response to another you need to ensure that there is no cross-contamination of scents, i.e. each item is clean apart from a single taught scent. Confusion caused by multiple scents will reduce reliability of indication. You also need to be a great trainer as this is extremely demanding on dog and handler and I've yet to see it done completely, e.g. dog finds one scent during the search and sits but when he finds another during the same search he retrieves it. If you manage this, I'd love to see the video.

The first step is to discover what your dog would like to hunt for, toys or food. Whichever one is chosen, the dog will be hunting for the scent not the article. This is an important point as some people get hung up on the, erroneous, thought that searching for food is easier or less 'valid' than searching for a non-food scent. The principal is exactly the same, no worse no better.

If your dog is a half-hearted toy tugger or a disinterested retriever, it is likely that he would be more motivated if he could search for food. The motivation for the search is the game at the end. But if the dog doesn't like the game at the end, the motivation to search is reduced. If the dog is an enthusiastic foodie, then the obvious reward at the end of the search is finding the food. My belief is that it is unfair and ridiculous to exclude dogs that don't enjoy games with toys from the joy of scentworking. So if your dog likes cheese more than chase, choose food. How to introduce food scent is explained later in this section.

ACTIVE INDICATION

Non-food searches

Once you know that your dog loves to play with toys, scent up your chosen article. For clarity and ease of writing I will talk about catnip as the scent and the mouse as the article as these are commonly used in my workshops.

Begin by playing with your dog and the catnip scented mouse. Make it a really exciting game, full of competition, energy and excitement. All the rules you might have heard about never playing tug, don't chase the dog, no teasing, all go out the window. Play the game your dog wants to play, give in to the fun. Then, when the game has reached it's peak and the dog is loving it, take the mouse away, put it in an unscented bag or container and place it somewhere that the dog cannot access it. The reason for this 'mean' act, is that you want the dog to associate the mouse with heaps of fun. By stopping the game at it's most exciting point, you prevent the dog from getting bored with the mouse and increase the desire for him to play with it again the next time he sees it.

After giving the dog a complete break from playing (all games, not just this one), a drink and a rest (you should both need it if the game was energetic enough), you are ready to start throw-ins. Throw-ins are the important link between playing with the catnip mouse and searching for it, and is generally done in three steps. If you have somebody to help you, they can tease the dog and toss the toy into the room for you at each step.

Throw-in: Step 1

Using the living room as the search area, have a short game with your dog and the mouse in the hall. Then hold your dog by the collar, run him to the living room door, throw the mouse straight into the room, release him as you say 'Find it', and follow him in so you can resume the exciting game with him and the mouse. Make this game intense but fairly short.

Let's think about what you've just done. First of all, you've reminded him that playing with the mouse is fun. Then, keeping up the energy of the game by running to the living room door, you've introduced a tiny bit of frustration by holding his collar. This helps him to jump into the search area with gusto much more than an energy-sapping sit-stay. The mouse is thrown dead ahead of the dog into the room. He needs to see it being thrown and see where it lands so that he knows exactly where to go to get it. In order to keep the energy up, the instant you throw it, give the search cue and let go of the collar. You've set the dog up for success, all you need to do now is run into the room with him to resume the game with the mouse as soon as your dog picks it up.

Throw-in: Step 2

Finish up the game from step 1, take the dog back into the hall, hold his collar and throw the mouse back into the living room. This time, instead of throwing it straight into the room, throw it to the side so that when the dog runs in he has to have a quick look to find it rather than it being straight in front of him. Once you've tossed the mouse to the side, give your 'Find it!' cue, and let the dog run in to grab the mouse. Follow him in as before and play with him and the mouse.

Throw-in: Step 3

Finish up the game from step 2 and take the dog back into the hall. Leaving the dog in the hall, you should take the mouse into the room, closing the door behind you. Place the mouse just behind something, such as a footstool, magazine rack or cushion on the floor. This should be placed just to the side as the dog comes into the room. You are sitting the mouse behind something more than hiding it at this point so don't make it too difficult for your dog to locate the mouse. In the previous two steps you have built up trust – when you say 'Find it!' there will always be a scented mouse to find, you will never trick him. So this time, when he sees you go into the room with the mouse but doesn't see you throw it, he can have trust that when you say 'Find it!', the mouse will be there somewhere. You are now ready to let the dog into the room. As you open the door, say 'Find it!', step back in the direction of the mouse. If your dog looks a little confused, say 'Find it!' again, moving towards and then past the mouse. Your movement should encourage the dog to move around too and then to catch a whiff, or even catch sight of, the mouse. When he finds it, have the biggest game ever.

After the third throw-in, finish the game. Put the mouse in a bag or container ready to be washed and rescented before using it again, or to help maintain the scent it already has on it if you plan to do some more work later the same day. Remember not to put it back into your storage tin. Doing so will contaminate the other articles, the catnip and the inside of the tin with both the dog's slobbery scent and the scent from your hands.

The purpose of the throw-ins is to gradually build the idea that the scented article is there to be found and played with by the dog. It's his introduction to searching for something. Don't worry that he is using his eyes on the first, second, and perhaps third, throw-in, he is learning to search so you need to set him up to succeed.

Food searches

The introduction to searching using food as the scent article is started a little differently. First you need to choose your food. Obviously it has to be something that you dog likes. My strong recommendation is to use cheese, just a value brand mild cheddar or similar. Cheese has some surprising properties. The main one is that it sticks to almost anything! This makes it fabulous for scentwork as you are less limited to where you can hide it than you are with a toy. You can stick cheese to walls, fences, furniture, boxes, cars (for vehicle searches), plastic, wood, the list goes on. In fact cheese will stick almost everything except cold metal. Your dog won't be eating huge quantities of cheese when searching so it shouldn't affect his weight or wellbeing. You can of course use other food, preferably something soft and smelly. Biscuits are not great for this stage of scentwork as they have a much smaller scent picture than cheese or other soft foods. Cheese can also be warmed in your hand and molded like plasticine. This further increases the scent picture and makes it easier for your dog to find.

If you are working indoors or are outdoors and your dog is safe to be loose, then do the following three exercises off lead. If you are in a class situation or in an area where your dog might be very distracted, work on lead.

Start by playing the 'Find it!' game.

Find it!

Cut some cheese into tiny pieces. Give your dog a piece of the cheese. Then throw the next piece onto the ground, close to where you are standing. As you throw the next piece say 'Find it', or whatever your scentwork word is going to be. From now on, whenever you toss a piece of cheese to the ground say 'Find it' as you throw it. This will prompt the dog to look down to start sniffing out the cheese. In other words, you are teaching the dog to scent on cue. What adds value to this game is that once the dog has eaten the tiny titbit of cheese, he will return to you to see if you are going to throw another piece. By waiting until he comes back to you, you are effectively rewarding a recall. More on this later. You can now start to toss the cheese further away, gradually increasing the distance the dog has to search. Then you can introduce some direction by throwing it to your, left, right or even behind you. Play this game for a minute or so and your dog will quickly learn that the 'Find it' game is one he'll want to play again and again.

Once he is happy to play the game, you can start to throw the food around corners and behind things. This increases the search time and helps him get used to finding the food in unexpected areas, such as behind the coffee table or under a chair.

If you do not intend to use scentwork as a team game, i.e. you watch the dog search for the cheese rather than actively helping him to find it, then you can stop at this stage. You have taught the find it cue and the dog has learned that he will be rewarded with the found cheese. Job done!

It's well worth highlighting the usefulness of this game for all dogs. I use the 'Find it!' game to reward recalls, help dogs cope with traffic, build confidence around strangers, prevent them from eating horse/rabbit/deer poo, move past not through muddy puddles and pay attention to me rather than other dogs. Even if your dog is scentworking for a non-food item, he can still play the 'Find it!' game with food. It is so adaptable and useful, a staple in my training toolbox.

'One you see, one you don't'

This next step teaches the dog the relevance of your hand gesture and lets him search for a titbit that he hasn't seen you throw.

Facing your dog and holding one titbit in each hand, throw one titbit to the left and ask your dog to 'Find it' as he runs to get it. Immediately as your dog turns to follow the first titbit, you throw the second titbit to the right. You can throw the first titbit a little further away than the second to give you more time to throw the second titbit without him seeing. But at this stage don't throw them too far. Remember that your goal is to help the dog succeed.

When the dog comes back after eating the first titbit, using your whole arm rather than just your index finger, sweep your hand towards the second titbit and encourage your dog to find it by saying 'Find it'. This nifty exercise teaches your dog to follow your hand direction, look to the ground and then get rewarded by finding a titbit. It also teaches him to trust that even if he doesn't know or think that there's something out there, he can trust you and follow your cue. Tricking him by gesturing in a direction where there is no treat will diminish trust between you and your dog. If you send your dog to find something he must have trust that you are not lying.

Throwing the first titbit, which essentially is just to distract the dog so that you can throw the second one unseen, to the left means that it is easy for you to give the directional hand signal to the right. As you begin to search, you will only be using your right hand to give direction to the dog, so now is a great time to practise this foundation skill. If the dog starts to specifically follow your hand rather than the direction it is showing, help your dog put his nose down by sweeping your hand along the ground, palm up, tapping the ground with the back of your fingers. As the dog puts his nose to the ground, you can sweep your hand out of the way and let him continue on in the direction of the cheese. Make sure you don't have any bits of cheese still in your hand or this will distract the dog from the search and encourage him to follow your hand directly.

As before, once your dog has the hang of this routine, you can gradually toss titbits further away, and introduce some direction. This increased distance and reduction in predictability encourages him to use his nose to find the food and to look to you for a hint about where to look, i.e. the sweeping gesture with your right hand.

Later, you can work in grass with small titbits to encourage the dog to really use his nose to find the reward.

As before, play this game for a short time, only a minute or two.

Drop and go back

This is the third part of the food introduction.

Encourage the dog to walk beside you on the left. As you walk drop a piece of cheese onto the floor with your right hand. Cheese is unlikely to roll and it's silent when you drop it so the dog won't be alerted to the fact that you've dropped anything. Continue walking for another 5 steps, then turn around to your right and encourage your dog to find it, using the same sweeping hand gesture and verbal cue 'Find it' as in the previous exercises. This teaches the dog to have faith and trust that whatever he's doing, if you cue 'Find it' there will always be something for him to find. It also helps you practise the sweeping hand gesture and helps him learn that it suggests a good place to search. As you turn and say 'Find it' your hand will sweep round to the right and towards the cheese. After a couple of tries, increase the distance you walk before turning round and sending your dog to 'Find it'.

If you try this with your dog on the right or if you turn to your left after you've dropped the cheese you'll get yourself, and your dog, tangled up in all sort of knots. Following the instructions I've given should result in a nice, smooth, flowing exercise.

Putting it all together

Having done all three exercises, you can now combine them to start a small search. Say 'Find it' and toss one piece of cheese just out of sight. Repeat this but do it in the style of 'One you see, one you don't'. Say 'Find it', toss one piece of cheese to the left and then immediately throw a second to the right, again just out of sight. When the dog finds the first one, you can send him to 'Find it' again, but use the sweeping hand signal to give him a clue to which direction he should go. Repeat this several times so that he is looking for the cheese with his nose, cued and guided by you.

If your dog is happy to have a slight delay in the reward, you can place the food inside containers that allow the scent to come out easily, such as plastic pipes with holes drilled into them. This is a great help if you are working alone as it stops the dog from finding and eating the food without you realizing it. The dog would bring the food filled container out of the hide and then you empty the food out of it for him. As with the dogs searching for non-food articles, you must ensure that you use a variety of containers so that the dog does not start to look for the container rather than the food.

Once you have completed all the steps to introducing your dog to the scent, food or non-food, let him rest. Scentwork is very mentally tiring so you do not want to push your dog too hard or try to make him learn too fast. Later, or even the following day, you can move to the next stage: first searches.

First Searches

The first search you'll do is the free search. This is when the dog is allowed to search the whole area with minimal guidance from you. You are there to encourage him to continue searching and to make sure he doesn't miss out any part of the area. Begin by hiding the scented mouse / cheese. Make sure that he can access the find when he locates it, you don't want him to find it but be unable to grab and play with it, or eat it in the case of cheese. So hide it at floor level, perhaps behind a chair or under a cushion on the floor. With the cheese you can stick it to a chair or table leg close to the ground.

While you are hiding the article, leave your dog outside the room, behind a closed door. When you are ready for him to search, go out to join him so that when you open the door you can send him into the room saying 'Find it' as you do. This search should be done in the same room that you used for the throw-ins or food games. The continuity of using the same area means that you are gradually layering up the dog's experiences, building on previous work little by little. Any changes can impede learning so it's important that only one thing is changed at a time, e.g. sending the dog to search when he can see the item being thrown into the room to not seeing it being thrown.

Open the door and immediately send your dog to 'Find it'. Sweep your right hand into the room, gesturing towards potential hiding places but not necessarily towards the actual hide at this stage. To give the inexperienced dog something definite to search, gesture close to, or even tap with the back of your fingers, a specific article, such as a box or chair, rather than waving your hand in mid air. Quickly move into the centre of the room, walking backwards so that you can watch the dog at all times during the search. You are watching for indications that your dog has found the scent and for any signs that he needs some help. While your dog is searching you can encourage him, 'good lad', but you don't want to distract or badger him by repeating the 'Find it' cue too often. As long as he is sniffing and searching, there's no need to repeat it. But when he lifts his head or looks at you, this is the right time to remind him to 'Find it' and give the hand gesture. This will motivate him to keep going, safe in the knowledge that he will find the article.

When you see any sort of indication, change in the dog's behaviour or demeanour, you should ask a question 'Have you got something?' This question will either prompt the dog to investigate further (yes, he thinks he's found something) or to move away to search somewhere else (no, he doesn't think it is there.) We all know how nosy dogs are, if we look at something they want to look at it too. Therefore, as you ask the question, you are going to step away from the dog. This allows him to answer the question honestly, without any influence from you, the handler. The simple act of stepping towards the dog as the question is asked can be enough to convince the dog that you know something he doesn't. So he looks more interested and you think yes, he's indicating more which makes you move even closer. This spiraling effect leads to a dead end with handler and dog persuading each other that they have found the hide. All well and good if they have found it, but if not, then the dog will be disappointed and you will question your interpretation of the indication.

You've asked the question 'Have you got something', stepped away as you've asked it, but your dog stays where he is, continuing to sniff and indicate. Now you can encourage him to get the find. 'Go on; you get it; sort it out; where is it?' He shouldn't need any physical assistance from you to reach the find as you will have placed it in easy reach for him. So when he gets it really show how pleased you are by praising him and playing an exciting game with the toy. After a short but enthusiastic game, take him from the room and hide the article again. If he has found the cheese, let him eat it and praise him up before taking him out so you can hide more cheese.

Hide the article as before but in a different place in the same room. Send him in saying 'Find it' as he goes in. Support him by moving around the room, repeating 'Find it' only if he looks up or at you. Then, spot the indication, ask the question, move away and get ready to play.

Obviously, if you are the person hiding the article, you know where it is. When you are searching, you should neither lead your dog to it nor completely avoid it. Pretend you have no idea where it is hidden and let your dog search freely around the room. If you lead him to it, he doesn't have the chance to search for himself and so won't have the fun of building up his scentwork skills and confidence. It also means that you won't be observing him carefully enough, looking for those precious indications that become even more sought after when you come to doing searches where you do not know where the article has been hidden. Likewise, if you avoid the area, he might miss it out completely and so the search will be too long and unrewarding.

If you have a willing assistant, they can hide the article. Give them clear guidelines as to where they should and should not place the article. And ask them to stay with you while you search so they can assist you and the dog should he need any help. For example, driving him into a blank area or inadvertently stepping forward as you ask the question resulting in false indications can be halted by the assistant telling you it's not there.

I advise only doing three or four short searches at this point. Your dog is building experience as well as concentration. Put the scented article in a ziplock bag or container, ready to be washed and re-scented before it is used again.

PASSIVE INDICATION

As with all dog training exercises, there are many ways to teach a passive response. I am going to detail two, one for dogs that prefer toy play as a reward and the other for dogs that prefer food rewards.

Method one – Toy reward

This is a variation of the method currently favoured by the UK Border Agency. This method teaches a stare indication. This does not require the dog to be in a specific position, such as sit or down, but simply requires that he stares at the source of the scent. A nice refinement gained by using this method is that the dog can indicate the height of the find by directing his stare to the exact scent source rather than simply sitting in proximity to it. This can be further exaggerated by the dog choosing to lie down to stare at a very low scent source, or stretching up to stare at a high find. The dog is not asked to adopt these positions. Instead he may opt for them as part of a natural but intense stare. When he gives the stare indication, he is rewarded with a tennis ball.

To begin this method, the dog must become obsessed by playing with a tennis ball. This must become his toy of choice, the one that he will work hard for, play with no matter what else is going on and not want to stop playing with when the game is over. This intense desire to play with the ball is what will motivate him to search long and hard. To help foster this positive obsession, you should engage your dog in fun playtimes with the ball making sure that you bring energy and excitement to the game. Then, once he adores the ball, limit access to all ball play so that it is a real treat when it comes out, something special that the dog does not have free access to at any other times. As you throw the ball for him, say 'Find it' so that he associates those words with the excitement of the tennis ball game.

You can then play the game in areas where you will want him to search. So, in a similar way to the initial throw-ins for the active indication, throw the ball into your hall so that it lands just out of sight, then send the dog in to find it. If your hall is clear, put out a couple of obstacles for the ball to hide behind, such as a cushion or a box.

Once you have cultivated this strong drive to play with the tennis ball, cut one up into tiny pieces, no bigger than 1cm. Make sure you have another tennis ball on you to use as the reward when your dog finds the tiny piece of cut up ball. You can carry one in your pocket but often it is difficult to get the ball out at just the right time. Much better to use a tennis ball clip or holder attached to your belt (the same ones used by tennis players.) Attach the ball clip to the back of your belt on the left side so that you can easily access it with your left hand (remember the right hand will be guiding the dog.)

Of key importance with the passive indication is that the dog never retrieves the article. He must not be able to pick it up. A neat trick to hide the piece of tennis ball is to wedge it in a door, either on the hinge side or the side that opens. Hence my recommendation to work in the hall where you are more likely to have access to more than one door. Close the door and just before it's fully shut, place the piece of tennis ball in the space between the frame and the door. As the door shuts it should keep the piece in place. When first placing the tennis ball sliver, place it just below your dog's nose level. This will make it easy for the dog to find. Unlike teaching the active indication, I recommend that you hide the articles for the initial searches, known searches. This way you should be able to clearly see exactly when the dog starts to indicate. Missing indications at this early stage can cause doubt and confusion later on. But beware and be honest with yourself, only react to indications, not simply to the dog's proximity to the article or a regular sniff at it. The dog needs to behave differently when he hits the scent. That indication is what you should react to, i.e. tossing him the ball, not you assuming that because he is near the source he can smell it.

Send your dog into the area, saying 'Find it' to let him know that his ball is in there somewhere. As he hits the scent of the ball on the door, ask the question 'Have you got something?' (more on this later) and when he indicates again by looking at the piece of tennis ball, reward him by swiftly and gently tossing the ball in front of the dog aiming at the spot where the tiny piece of ball is hidden. Too hard a throw may startle the dog and cause the ball to bounce away from the spot. Tossing the ball directly at the area where the dog correctly indicated will reinforce the association with finding the scent of the ball and the game with the ball, and will encourage the dog to stare at the correct area rather than looking back at you. The dog indicates that he has found the scent by staring at it. He may lie down as the scent source will be placed below the height of his nose. This is fine. The position he adopts is not the important factor. He just needs to be staring at it. If your aim is not good, practise tossing the ball at a target without your dog being present. Repeat the routine of hiding a piece of the ball and rewarding at the scent source with the ball when he indicates two or three more times, then end the session.

Practise this routine in several different locations around your home/hall so that the dog starts to check all the doors and other areas you might find to hide the sliver of tennis ball - he must not be able to retrieve the sliver.

After approximately six sessions of several searches at a time (some dogs need more sessions, but don't do less), you can introduce the actual scent that you would like your dog to find, for example catnip. Add catnip to the container that holds the pieces of tennis ball and leave it overnight so that the tennis ball pieces absorb the scent of the catnip. At your next training session, return to the area where you did your initial searches. Hide a piece of the catnip scented tennis ball in the door, just as before, then send your dog in to 'Find it.' At this point in the game, your dog will still be searching for the scent of the tennis ball but he will discover that it also comes with another scent, the catnip. As before, when he hits the scent of the ball on the door, ask the question 'Have you got something?' and when he indicates again by looking at the piece of tennis ball, reward him by swiftly and gently tossing the ball in front of the dog aiming at the spot where the tiny scented piece of ball is hidden. Hide the scented slivers a few times, then end the session. Everything about this session is the same as the previous ones, dog finds tennis ball piece, indicates, is rewarded with a tennis ball. Except now he has an additional scent that is becoming associated with the game.

When working with your passive indicating dog, your handling skills are the same as those for the active indication. The main difference in these early stages is that the dog is searching along walls and doors rather than anything in the middle of the room. Therefore your handling style should be more like the directed searches, walking back, guiding with your right hand, being methodical. The searches should be very short, really just covering a short length of around 6ft/2m maximum. Later, as the dog gains in experience, you can widen the search areas so that he is working the free search, and patterns the same as the active dogs. Working a more directed search style helps reduce boisterous activity at these early stages and helps foster good concentration, which is needed when looking for smaller scent articles. But beware, this instant concentration can be too demanding for some dogs, so always watch for signs of stress or frustration, such as stopping the search to have a scratch, yawning or solicitous approaches to you instead of working the area. If the dog wants to work in a very wide area, you can do this on lead. But if you can avoid this during these early stages you will avoid inadvertently crowding or pressuring your dog.

Just as with active indications, you ask 'Have you got something?' when the dog indicates. Step away as you ask, just as you would for a dog giving an active indication. The difference now, is that if the dog has found the scent source, he should continue to stare at it. You do not drive him in, you simply deliver the ball. If he moves away, continue searching.

The next step is to replace the pieces of catnip scented tennis ball with small pieces of fabric scented with catnip. The purpose of this step is to concentrate the dog's search on catnip, which you can later apply to anything, rather than on the tennis ball scent. His reward history of finding the scent and being rewarded with the ball should have built trust between you and the dog. Every time he finds the source, he is guaranteed to be rewarded with the ball. Keep the search simple, set him up for success and be ready to reward him when he indicates on the catnip. So when he indicates on the catnip, ask 'Have you got something?', step away and reward as usual. After a couple of searches just using catnip you will have successfully changed him from finding the tennis ball scent to the catnip scent. He will still have the knowledge and skill to find tennis balls, once he has learned something he cannot unlearn it. But since all tennis balls and tennis ball material toys will have been removed from the area (this should be done as matter of course for passive dogs) and will no longer be provided as a search item, his skill in finding it will not be enhanced. Instead, the catnip scent will build a long, strong history and so can be used in the most challenging searches.

From here, you can develop the challenge of the searches just as you would for the dogs giving active indications.

Note
If the dog will happily work to find a scent, but prefers to be rewarded with food, you can toss food towards the scent source, just as you would the tennis ball. However, I do not recommend teaching the passive indication with food items as the scent unless you are prepared to work hard to ensure the dog cannot self-reward by licking the food even if he can't get it all by himself.

Method two – Food reward
I recommend using a clicker or clicker word to teach this method. This gives the dog very clear feedback and helps you to time your rewards well. Using this method, it is likely that the dog will look at you more than at the exact location of the find. He will look at you when you click in expectation of getting the treat. If you have a dog who is not already clicker trained, you can work more of a stare element into the indication by clicking and tossing the food towards the hide (as you'd do with the non food method described previously.) But the clicker gives a nice, definite, accurate response to the indication which helps build confidence and reliability.

Begin by presenting the dog with the scent in a glass jar with multiple holes in the lid (make sure the holes are made by pushing the screwdriver or other implement into the lid so that the sharp edges are on the inside, don't want your dog to cut his nose!) Many dogs, unless trained to do so, are less likely to pick up glass than other objects such as cardboard boxes. At this early stage in training, you want the dog to smell the scent without him being tempted to pick up the jar. So hold it in your hand rather than sitting it on the floor. Offer the scented jar towards the dog so that he sniffs it. When he sniffs it, click and treat. You are building an association between the scent and the reward. Move the scent so that it's offered from the left, the right, from below and above, clicking and treating every time the dog takes a sniff. As he learns to sniff the scent when it's offered, you can introduce the cue to find, so say 'Find it' as you offer him the scent. The next step is to make a subtle change in the routine. Hold the scented jar so that the dog has to come towards it to sniff it, rather than you offering it towards him. Say 'Find it', then click and treat when he moves forward and gives it a sniff.

Next you need to build in a trained response to the scent. My recommendation is to choose the position that comes most naturally to your dog, usually sit or lie down. For many dogs, sit will be the most appropriate. If your dog does not lie down when asked, then sit will be the indication of choice. But if your collie, for example, prefers to lie down, go with it. Cue the search, offer the dog the scent, but this time when he sniffs it, ask for the indication position before clicking. So, say 'Find it', offer the scent, dog sniffs, ask the dog to sit, click & treat. To begin with you will need to ask the dog to sit. He won't automatically know that you want him to sit when he smells a particular scent so you need to teach him the desired response. A lovely way to enhance the sit is to practise just the sit before you bring out the scented jar. If sit was the last thing he practiced, he is more likely to offer it up now. You go back to offering the scented jar to the dog because you have introduced a new element, the sit. As one part of the sequence gets harder, you compensate by making another part easier.

You need to practise in short but frequent sessions, building to the point where the dog automatically sits when he smells the scent. To ensure he is sniffing the scent before he sits and not taking you holding the scented jar as a cue to sit, return to putting the jar on the ground, then on a chair, on a low table, etc. so that the dog gets to go and sniff the jar when it's not in your hand. Stand fairly close to the jar as a way of encouraging your dog to go close enough to sniff it, and remember to cue the search by saying 'Find it' as he comes into the room. If he is sniffing but not sitting, click & treat the sniff, then cue the sit, which you also click & treat. Should he need it, you can use the hand gesture, as described in the active indication section, to suggest a direction for the dog to sniff. Use a variety of jars so that you ensure the dog is indicating on the scent inside the jar, not just the jar itself. The jar is likely to become contaminated with your smell and the smell of the treats you are using just by you handling it, so wipe it down with an unscented antibacterial wipe or liquid after every training session.

This is advanced training and should not be rushed. Any negativity, pressure or uncertainty from the handler will be detrimental to the learning process. This complicated exercise requires calm, supportive, knowledgeable handling as the dog has a lot to think about.

Once you can sit the jar down and the dog will rush to find and indicate at it, and is sitting automatically, you can move to the next stage, which is hiding the jar. Just as I described with the active indication, start by placing the jar in fairly easy hides, behind furniture, under cushions or newspapers or behind doors. When the dog finds the scented jar, he should sit. If he finds the jar but doesn't sit, click & treat, then ask him to sit and click & treat that. Hide the scented jar again, in a similar place, and this time when he finds the jar, you can say 'Good' but don't click & treat, just wait a few seconds to see if he offers the sit. When he does, click and jackpot, which means that you give him a whole handful of treats rather than just one. Repeat the search, wait for the sit, click & treat. If the dog isn't sitting automatically, go back to the step where he can see the jar and work on his sit response there.

Once you have a reliable indication on a hidden jar, you can continue to develop the challenge of the searches just as you would for the dogs giving active indications.

Part 6

Search Specifics

STARTER SEARCHES

To begin with, searches should only last seconds. From the brief search during the third throw-in lasting a few seconds to advanced searches lasting 30+ minutes, there are many steps to take. The length of the search depends on the dog's stamina, concentration and confidence, all of which must be advanced gradually. Placing finds in impossible locations, reducing the scent picture and searching for too long in the early stages of scentwork will decrease the dog's confidence and instead of rushing forward, you could grind to a halt.

Initial searches should be nice and straightforward. Limit the number of things in the area that could distract the dog. The more there is in the area the more there is for the dog to search. At my workshops I limit the number of boxes I put out in the search area so that the dog only has to search a maximum of six or so before he finds the article. Searches do not always go to plan. You might think you'll give the dog a nice quick find, but if he doesn't search that particular box or area first, he might have to search all the rest before he comes to it. As the handler, your job is to gently guide him towards the hide when appropriate. Rather than letting him struggle or risk him becoming frustrated, guide him towards the hide and suggests he searches there, simply by moving towards it and using the hand gesture. You may also repeat 'Find it' if you think he needs that extra encouragement to keep working. When he does locate and indicate on the find, you can ask the question 'Have you got something?', stepping away as you do so ready for him to pull it out and have a game with you. Each time you suggest looking somewhere and he is successful as a result of your help, the dog learns that you can be a real asset to the search. This gives great support to inexperienced dogs or those lacking general confidence, but also help confident, independent dogs to pay attention to you. Independent dogs can start out by ignoring the handler, just searching alone. While this is fine for owners who do not wish to participate in the search apart from hiding the article, for those who want to work with their dog and move on to more challenging searches, it is essential that the dog views you as a team mate, a helper. As the challenge of the searches becomes greater, you can work on this aspect of scentwork, encouraging the dog to pay attention to your suggestions.

This assistance should not be confused with the handler telling the dog where the find is or looking for it themselves in blind searches. You've heard the phrase "Why have a dog and bark yourself?" Well why have a dog and search yourself? Taking a dog to the find means that the dog doesn't have to search, he has you to do it for him. This means that in blind searches where neither of you know where it is he will have trouble locating it and won't be able to rely on you to find it. So suggest he looks somewhere then look for his indication. No indication, no find. The more often you can get somebody else to hide the article the better as it keeps you watching the dog, working with him. If you know where it is, it can be difficult to accurately identify indications. You may think you see a change because the dog is close to the hide, but is he really indicating? And it is for this reason that I prefer to use blind searches, where the handler does not know where the hide is, when first teaching scentwork. This is not always practical, e.g. if you are working alone, but just be alert to the danger of assuming you see things when you don't, and, equally, of avoiding areas for fear of leading the dog directly to the hide. Just work the dog as if you do not know where the hide is and be guided only by his indications not by your assumptions.

At this stage in training, he should find something at every search. Short searches with quick finds. Remember to play a good game with the find, or help the dog get all the cheese out of the box. If you skimp on the reward, the search may go downhill.

As the dog becomes more proficient, you can start to search in a variety of areas. So if you've been searching the living room, why not search the hallway or the dining room? Then you can link them all together and search the living room and the hall and/or the dining room. You are increasing the search time as the dog's concentration and search stamina increases. Introduce hides at different heights. Put the find on top of the radiator (switched off) or behind the curtain on the windowsill. Encourage your dog to use you to lean on so that if he gets up on his hind legs he can rest his front legs on you while he looks at height. Some dogs are unwilling to do this, mostly if they have been taught not to jump up on people, so it's no problem to let them lean on the wall, radiator, etc. Just think about where you do and do not want your dog to go. If you do not want him jumping up on furniture, don't hide it behind the cushions of the sofa. If you don't want to encourage counter surfing, don't hide it on the kitchen worktops. Be sensible and practical. Consider the safety of the area you are searching. Cables from lamps, the TV or the computer are easy for the dog to get tangled in, so don't place the find amongst them or encourage your dog to search them if you don't want to risk the dog breaking anything or getting a fright as he pulls a lamp off the table. Think also about chemicals and cleaners. These are most often found in the kitchen, bathroom and outdoor areas such as sheds and garages. Make sure they are safely out of reach or choose not to search in certain areas. For example, even though I know that dogs will ignore food while searching for other scents, I don't want to encourage my dog to work in the kitchen so that room is out of bounds for me as a search area. Set your search areas according to safety and preference.

Tip:
Make a note of where and when you hid articles to ensure you are not hiding articles in the same places all the time. It also helps to know where previous hides were in case your dog indicates on them when there is nothing (except residual scent) there.

INTERMEDIATE SEARCHES

Stepping up the challenge of the search is about increasing the search time, adding more elements to the search such as height and reducing the scent picture so that the dog has to work hard to locate the find. I advise that if you've not already done so, that you start working your dog in a harness. You need to be able to support him at height or when searching anything unsteady. Also, working on lead directed searches, any restriction of the throat or head will affect the efficiency of the dog's search. So working him on a harness instead of a headcollar or collar is recommended. I currently recommend the working dog harness by Catac, the same one as currently used by the UK Border Agency. They are simple, strong and do not have handles or back pads that can all too easily get caught up when the dog is working. I particularly like the wide girth strap, which comes with either a clip closure or a leather buckle strap. The width allows for more comfort when the dog's weight is being taken by the harness, such as when he's jumping off things and you support his weight through the harness to protect his shoulders and elbows as he lands.

Begin by putting out 2 finds. This will allow you to keep searching the area after the first find is located. When the dog brings out the first find, have a very brief game, dispose of the find, either to your back pocket or out of the search area, and carry on the search. Some dogs are a little perplexed when this first happens as they have found the find and have no idea there is another one out there. However, if you encourage them to search on and then they find the second one, their faith in you increases. You suggested they search on and when they did they found something else, brilliant, you just increased your value as a team member. If the dog indicates on a previous hide, tell him he's a good lad, i.e. acknowledge his correct indication, and then work him on. As your search area increases, you can put out several finds, working him on from each one after a brief game.

Introduce height in a similar way. Suggest the dog looks in an area he hadn't previously considered searching, and bingo! he finds the article. A rich source of equipment for use in scentwork is your local stationery shop. They have all sorts of clips and hooks that you can use to loosely attach the article to the back of curtains, chairs, clothes, etc. They also have magnetic clips that you can use for vehicle searches or anywhere with a metal surface that would be a suitable hide. They also have pencil cases inside which you can place the article (provides one more layer for the scent to get through) or use as the article. Such a variety of materials including cloth, fake fur, plastic and rubber makes for a diversity of challenges, both in the location of the find and in the retrieve aspect of the search. Bags and clothes hanging on the back of chairs or on hooks on the wall can be useful hides too. Do not hang things on coat stands or other free standing items as these are likely to be pulled over by active indicating dogs. Passive indicating dogs are fine with them. Think carefully about placing finds in clothing. These can be great places to hide things but it will encourage the dog to search clothes and they may get ripped or damaged when the dog is retrieving the find. I like to use clothes that would be otherwise be thrown away rather than any I would want to wear again.

Height is very easy to achieve if you are using cheese because it sticks to most surfaces. You can stick a piece under the windowsill, on the door, on the banister, under the car, beside the bin, on the fence. Cheese is super flexible when used this way.

When introducing height, ensure that the article is within the dog's reach. If he starts air scenting during the free search, verbally encourage him to follow his nose. Ask ' Have you got something?' and as he sticks to the air scent, gently praise him and support him, 'Good lad, you get it, where is it, clever dog.' If he doesn't hit the scent during the free search, then when you are working the perimeter and the inside of the area, suggest he looks higher when he is close to the hide. Suggesting height when he is far from the article can be counter-productive as he will not find anything and so could quickly dismiss your suggestion to look higher up as pointless.

Once he has found something higher up, he will be keener to look high himself as well as at your suggestion. Over the next few searches, have one hide high and one lower during each search so that he gets rewarded for checking high, but doesn't forget to check low. When introducing height it's also worth considering very low hides. During the initial searches, finds are often at the dog's nose level. Now is the time to start placing them even lower, under mats, under boxes, on skirting boards (cheese.) This greater variety of hides keeps the searches fun while increasing the challenge for the team. Ultimately, everywhere could be a potential hide. Ceilings, behind furniture, in wall or flooring cavities, dado rails, windows, curtains, books, anywhere!

Vehicle searches (exterior of vehicle)

These are great intermediate searches as they are done outdoors and so make a great introduction to this new area. Outdoor searches are more challenging due to the increased and sometimes more erratic airflow, hence why they are not great for initial searches. For example, you could be searching a car where the hide is on the back left wheel on the passenger side. The wind could easily bring the scent under the car so that the dog hits it on the other side, or at the front of the car. Then it is down to the handler spotting the indication, asking the questions, and allowing the dog, confident in his abilities, to trace the scent back to the source even though this means breaking away from the search pattern.

In essence, the vehicle search is simply an on lead directed search. As with any search, you want to use a pattern to help avoid any confusion and ensure that everything has been searched properly. I recommend starting the search at the driver's door, just behind the wing mirror. This means that if you were to move on to doing interior vehicle searches, you could work your way around the car and then when you get back to the driver's door, that's when you'd open it to let the dog inside. Work around the car, moving anti-clockwise so that your guiding right hand is closest to the car with your left holding the lead long and loose. Stand close to the vehicle and move at the dog's pace around it.

Before you commence the vehicle search, you have to set some limits. You do not want the dog to jump onto the paintwork. Therefore, finds must be placed in, on and around areas where the dog cannot do any damage. These areas include the wheels, hubcaps, wheel arches, bumpers or areas underneath the car. There are lots of little lips under the bodies of most vehicles when you can sit or stick articles. Also, you don't want the dog sniffing anything noxious or harmful, such as the petrol tank or a hot exhaust. Operationally, petrol tanks are often adapted by smugglers so the dog would be allowed to sniff the opening of the tank as well as all around it. But for our purposes this is not appropriate, both for the welfare of the dog and the fun of the search. The lead will help you move your dog away from jumping up at first and also keep him safe should you be working in a carpark or near a road on your driveway.

The first search should provide the dog with a quick, easy find. Place the article on the top of the tyre, driver's side, front. This means that when your dog gives you that puzzled look, as if to say, "Why are we standing beside our car, where are we going?", and "Did I hear you right, did you just say 'Find it!'?", you can quickly let him see the relevance of searching the car. Once he realizes that mice, cheese, etc. can be found on the car too, he'll be ecstatic. The first search should only take you from the bottom of the driver's door, to the wheel arch to the tyre. For the next search, put the find slightly further round the car so that the dog searches about half of it. And then finally, you can put the article even further around the car so the dog searches nearly all of it. Once you've done this, you can put a couple of articles out in the same search, so that the dog finds the first one, then keeps working on until he locates the second one at which point he has his big game. As with all directed searches, when the dog indicates, you still step away and ask 'Have you got something?' You can also let the dog push past you if he's picked up the scent, taking a mental note of the point in the search where he broke off so that if he cannot track down the source of the scent (it may have been carried away when the wind direction changed, or it may be scattered due to blustery conditions), you can go back to that point to resume the search. That way, nothing gets missed.

Once the dog realises that the vehicle is one big hide, he will be keen to get working. You may find on subsequent vehicle searches, that you do one circuit of the car almost as a free search, and then concentrate on the more detailed directed search on the second circuit.

Vehicle searches are so fascinating because of the air flow around, under and over the car. They really test the handler's skill in reading the dog, and the dog's skill on actually tracing the scent to the source.

Vehicle search (interior of vehicle)

As a general rule, I do not recommend interior vehicle searches unless you have access to vehicles other than your own. The residual scent of the article within the car will remain for some time. So, as is likely, if the dog travels in your car but smells his scentwork scent every time he goes in it, the scent will start to lose it's potency. It won't be as exciting to him because he can smell it but there is no search, no game, no reward for identifying it. Then there is the safety aspect. You do not want to encourage your dog to jump around inside the car, whether or not it is stationary. This will be messy and unsafe. And may ruin your dog's great settle in the car when you leave him in there while at a dog show or visiting a friend. Once he knows he's allowed to search it and go wherever her likes, it's difficult for him not to do it at will.

But, if you know someone who works on cars or has access to scrap cars, then go for it! Watch out for smashed glass, sharp edges and unstable floors, seats, shelves, etc. by ensuring you always do your safety check before commencing the search.

Search the exterior first, then let your dog into the car. Before starting the search, decide if the boot space is going to be part of the exterior or interior search. Saloon car boots are usually best done during the exterior search. If the parcel shelf is in place, hatchback and estate boots can be done during the exterior search. Otherwise they can easily be accessed from inside during the interior search. Do not put the dog in on top of a parcel shelf as it is likely to break, or startle the dog if it unexpectedly (to him) gives way under his weight. If the dog is keen to get into the car during the exterior search, i.e. he is indicating strongly that the article is inside the car, then let him in (keeping a mental note of how much of the exterior has still to be searched.) Unless you are searching trailers, caravans or limousines, it is unlikely that there will be enough space in the car for you and your dog. Therefore you direct him from the outside of the car, leaning in and suggesting places for him to look. Try to be methodical, searching the front then the back. This plan can quickly come apart if the dog indicates early on in the search but then has to track back to the source. Help him track back, use the drive in technique using your voice to urge him on, and help him thoroughly investigate areas where he is indicating the most.

Interior car searches can be difficult due to the small area the dog has to work in and the high chance of the scent picture being fairly big, certainly during intermediate searches. Until the door is opened, the scent pools in the car and so the whole of the interior smells good to the dog. When everything smells of the scent it can be tricky to work through the scent picture to get to the source. The dog will really need the handler to help him find it.

Baggage searches

Operational baggage searches take many forms. They can be done on the baggage belt that ferries the bags around the carousel from airside to the arrivals hall. They can be done by searching the bags in the pods that bring the bags from the aircraft; they can be lined up as they are unloaded from the pods but before they are put onto the baggage belt; they can be specifically done on hand baggage where selected travelers line their bags up in front of them; and they can even be done without you knowing, just by the dog team walking through the arrivals lounge, departure lounge (especially if looking for money), the railway platform or the ferry terminal.

Some of these scenarios are easier for you to recreate than others!

Start by putting a selection of empty bags in a line on the floor. You can use handbags, suitcases, sport bags, satchels, bags made of leather, canvas, hessian, plastic. Hard shell cases and briefcases, such as Samsonite, are much more difficult for the dog to work, so leave them out of the searches for now. Leave enough space between the bags for the dog to walk around them and to ensure they are not touching. Remember that each new search type provides it's own challenges and so should be set up to allow the dog to be successful. If, at this stage of baggage searching, the bags are touching, it can be more difficult for the dog to identify which bag contains the article as both bags could easily become contaminated. Ideally, start baggage searches on lead to help focus the dog on searching just the bags not the whole room. As with the car search, you can quickly walk around the line of cases, as in a free search. However, if your dog is quickly settling into searching, you can go straight into a directed search. Work backwards, moving anti-clockwise around the line of bags so that your guiding hand is closest to the bags. Let the dog have a good sniff at each bag. If they want to walk over the top of them that's fine, it helps push the air through the bag and so increase the size of the scent picture. As the dog works the line of bags, if he shows any interest or gives any indication, ask the usual question 'Have you got something?' and back away. If he has and remains with the bag, help him to precisely locate the find by opening the bag and/or turning it over to allow him to access the article. If the dog is worried about putting his head into the bag or has trouble locating the find in the first place, you can start by hiding the article under rather than inside the bag.

If the dog doesn't indicate on any of the bags, help him search more thoroughly by turning the bags over, perhaps even opening them a little so he can have an extra good sniff. Don't be tempted to look into the bags yourself as you open them up, the dog will find the article, just give him time and opportunity.

Once you have used a bag, you can perhaps use it again for one more search, but then it needs to be washed. Chuck it in the washing machine at 60° to get rid of the smell of you and of the dog. There is likely to still be some residual smell of the scent you want your dog to find, but it will be very mild. However, do not hide a different scent in that bag, only ever use it with the original scent. Mixing the smell of more than one scent will diminish the dog's ability to accurately identify one particular scent.

Mix the order of the bags up between each search so that the dog doesn't have a preconceived idea of which bag it's in.

You can source bags to use in your searches by asking friends and family, checking out your local car boots and jumble sales and by going to auction houses and lost property offices.

Outdoor searches

As discussed in the car search section, working outdoors increases the environmental challenge and decreases the control you have over the temperature, wind direction and other distractions. Start by defining the area you intend to search. Look for landmarks to form boundaries, be they fences, a tree, a plantpot or a path. Be prepared for your dog to range more widely than with indoor searches. Allow him this wide range but don't follow him out of the designated search area. By allowing him to range out you give him the opportunity to maximise his use of wind direction (he will naturally use that to his advantage) and hopefully get a whiff of the desired scent. But by staying within the search area yourself, you can draw him back in order to follow the scent he's caught on the wind back to source and to minimise wasted energy spent searching outside the area.

As with the first car search, your dog will not be expecting to find his scent article in this new area. Areas where the dog has a reward history or strong expectation of doing a particular activity add an extra element to the initial searches. He needs to trust that when you give the search cue, 'Find it!', no matter where he is, he can be guaranteed to find his article. But that trust doesn't come cheap, so when he gives you the benefit of the doubt and starts to search outdoors, it is essential to ensure that he gets a quick easy find. This will reward his trust in you and reinforce the connection between following the search cue and finding the article.

Before placing the hide, check the area for holes, glass, debris, etc. so that neither the dog nor you get injured. When working outdoors, you won't be working backwards as it's all too easy to trip or fall over. Covering larger areas means that working backwards is not practical. Instead you'll be mostly walking forwards and sideways, with some backwards movement, so that you can observe the dog and watch where you are going. Check what can move and what cannot, such as unstable logs, industrial machinery or vehicles (such as those found on farms or haulage yards), fixtures and fittings in dilapidated areas. Never assume, always check for hazards before the search commences.

Outdoor searches give lots of scope for hides. In trees and bushes, under pots, logs or undergrowth, behind rocks and boulders, down ditches, in the sand and along the hedge. Safety is your primary concern, followed by access for the dog. Do not hide the article somewhere that you cannot access – you do not want the dog to get stuck somewhere that you cannot help him, so don't throw the article into a tiny space behind buildings or far into the undergrowth. Also, don't hide it in brambles, nettles or other plants that could injure your dog. Think about the weather conditions. Hot, dry weather will give larger scent pictures than damp, cold conditions. Wind is the main factor to consider. If you start your search upwind of the hide, the scent may be carried towards the dog and so give him the chance of an early indication. Downwind hides, where the scent will be carried away from the dog, may require more detailed searching or else the dog may run on ahead until he is upwind of the hide and so work back. This is why you need to be on your toes, thinking all the time about the scent picture and why your dog is searching in particular ways, e.g. ranging wide, moving away from the hide or working slowly.

An interesting aspect to working outdoors is that the dogs hit scent, or vapor, trails left by you/your assistant, as you walk along holding the scented article. Vapour trails are specifically targeted by some firearms and explosives (FX) detector dogs in areas such as airports, where criminals have explosives on their body or in their baggage. As they move through the airport, the dog picks up the trail and tracks it right to the criminal. I have seen dogs go straight to the article in some pretty challenging environments simply because they followed the vapour trail. To minimise this, and make the search more of a challenge, carry the article inside the sealed tin or container, only taking it out when you come to the spot where you want to hide it. Alternatively, you can walk around the area, stopping at several spots before actually placing the article so that even if the dog picks up the trail, he is not taken immediately to the hide. Of course, if your dog needs some help during outdoor searches, you can use the trail as a great asset.

Postal searches

Postal searches with pet dogs have been extremely enlightening for me. It made me appreciate just how good my, and all the Customs dogs, were. Postal searches involve the dog searching postal sacks full of mail. Sounds simple enough. However, let's break this down to consider some of the factors involved.

1. The postal sack itself – these are mostly made of woven propylene. These sacks appear to hold the scent of everywhere they've been and everything they've touched. I assume this is due to the weave rather than the propylene. Woven fabrics capture and retain scent in all the tiny gaps within the weave. If using used sacks, the combination of all the scents on the sacks can prove a challenge in themselves, never mind once they contain post and a scented article.

2. The contents – not every piece of post is the same when it comes to scent. I tend to split the post into three categories:

   a. paper envelopes – the easiest to search when the bag is not very full, allows the scent to move through the envelope quickly. Cheap envelopes (e.g. the brown ones that bring bills) are easier for the scent to move through and soak into than high quality thick envelopes (e.g. wedding invitations or embossed paper.) However, when densely packed into a postal bag, envelopes can hold and retain scent very effectively when sandwiched between many other envelopes without much movement.

b. small packets, boxes, padded envelopes – small cheap cardboard boxes will let the scent soak into them and will release it easily, just as with the cheap envelopes. Lots of boxes within a bag can make for a nice, intermediate challenge. By adding padded envelopes (plastic bubble wrap encased in shiny paper that holds the scent inside) you increase the difficulty.

c. shiny, printed leaflets, flyers, junk mail – this is the trickiest as the shiny material takes time to soak up the scent. It holds it in place so it can easily trap the scent between leaflets and flyers making it very difficult for the dog to find. This is especially true when the bag is densely packed with junk mail.

The simplest way to begin is by laying out a row of empty sacks, about 5 or 6. Hide the article under, not in, one of the sacks. Using the on lead directed search technique, work your way along the bags, around the top and back down them. Give the dog lots of time to have a good sniff and then make sure you have a really good game with him at the end when he finds the article. Once you've done a few successful postal searches you can put the article inside the otherwise empty sack, tipping it on end for the article to fall out when the dog gives a solid indication on the correct bag. This search is a lot like the baggage search in style and technique, such as moving the bags around (to help 'puff' out the scent) or turning them over for your dog to search more thoroughly.

After the initial session with empty bags, you can start adding some envelopes. Add envelops to all the bags so that they are all the same. Then put the article into the sack with the envelopes at first, only progressing to putting the article inside and envelope inside the bag once your dog is confidently searching the bags and indicating on the correct one. Gradually increase the number of envelopes, and boxes you add to the bags. You can also increase the number of bags. Remember, once a bag has contained the article it is contaminated. So this bag, and it's contents can only be used again if the article is hidden in it. And even then it should only be used a couple of times so that any other contamination, usually from the dog, is not associated with the article. These bags wash very well at 60° which should bring the level of contamination down to a minimum and so let you use them again.

When the dog indicates on the correct sack, you can tip the contents out and allow him to search through them to locate the article. This means that you can do two searches in one, i.e. one to identify the correct bag and a second to identify the correct envelope. If the dog cannot locate the correct envelope help him perform a systematic search of the envelopes. One method is to move them into a line along which the dog can search.

The search becomes more challenging as you increase the number of bags and the number of envelopes and boxes in the bags. Do not decrease the amount of scent at this juncture. That can be done later when the dog is confidently and successfully searching the postal sacks.

You can source postal sacks from your local post office, sometimes your postman can help you out. Or you can buy unused sacks, not necessarily postal, e.g. hessian sacks, from many gardening shops and online.

People searches (passive indication only)

One search the active dogs cannot do is people searches. Obviously you do not want to encourage your dog to jump onto people to retrieve the article, so a passive indication is required for this type of search.

Begin by sitting four or five people in a row. The dog should have access all around them, i.e. he should be able to walk around the row in front and behind the chairs. Having the people sit down makes them less intimidating, more inviting. One person should hide the scented article under their trouser leg. This means it is out of sight but still easily accessible for the dog. Ideally, they could stuff it into their sock. Working the dog on lead, as you would do for a car search, begin at one end of the line and, walking backwards to keep an eye on the dog, encourage him to search the people. Some very well trained and polite dogs can find this rather perturbing, having been taught not to sniff people. But with some encouragement and the excitement of the find, the dog should quickly realize that when cued to 'Find it' no matter what the item or area, he is allowed to search. Work along the line, then round the back in one big loop. As with any directed search, the dog may need to take one walk round as his free search, so the second walk around can be more concentrated. Other dogs start concentrating immediately and don't need a free search. When the dog hits the scent, he should sit. If he hits it and looks at you, say 'Have you got something?', then wait to see if he will offer the sit. Each new search requires the dog to generalize his previous training. So if he needs a little help or time, give it to him.

How to make the search thorough without repeating yourself

One of the most common handler errors I see as teams increase the search challenges, is lack of attention to detail. Not being thorough can make the difference between finding the article and missing it. But how to do that without going over and over the same area? As ever, the answer is simple: watch the dog. Really look at where he is sniffing. Look to see if he runs past the area or if he actually works it. Does he physically move into the space but mentally is engaged somewhere else? To help the dog pay attention to all the details practice directed searches where the hides are dotted in and around the areas most likely to be missed during searches. These are often the corners, various heights (if you and the dog have been searching high, the low parts of the search can be skimmed or missed, and vice versa.) Not moving/lifting/opening items that hold scent in rather than allowing a free flow of air is part of making the search thorough. Overall, the most common mistake is for the handler to assume that the hide could not be in a particular place and so actively avoids it. Scent can be anywhere, it's not the handler's job to find it. It is the handler's job to give the dog access to everything in order to ensure the area has been searched once, thoroughly. Setting a time limit on searching an area can be a good way to discipline yourself to being thorough and efficient. Repeatedly going over areas or items can turn the dog off. More and more I observe dogs who are very well aware that they have already searched and dismissed something. Asking them to search it again can be demoralizing for both members of the team. And remember to split the search area into manageable sections. Several smaller searches within the search area allow you to complete each section then forget all about it, keeping your mind free to fully concentrate on the next section.

ADVANCED SEARCHES

At this stage you are providing the dog with very challenging searches. For some dogs, this is a step too far. Dogs who can successfully work at this advanced level need to be confident, have a strong drive to work and trust the handler to support them. If you find that your dog's motivation to search starts to drop as the searches become more difficult, go back to the last level that the dog enjoyed and work on providing variety at that level and below.

Advanced searches minimize the scent picture. This can be done by having very small scented articles, such as scraps of material, small pieces of plastic piping, lagging and, ultimately, just smearing the scent onto surfaces or using labels to stick into and onto areas. Small amounts of scent give off less smell and make smaller scent pictures, thus are harder to locate. Alternatively you can hide larger articles deeper within hides, so inside boxes inside boxes, wrapped up, inside plastic and wood, deep inside full postal bags or suitcases containing clothes. The better you understand scent and how it moves the more insight you will have into the level of difficulty you are presenting to your dog.

The handler's role is heightened at this level too. Thorough searches are essential, don't skip areas, cut corners or assume that there is no hide anywhere. Smearing scent or using labels or slips of paper inserted into cracks will often not be visible so make no assumptions, search everything.

When searching for pure scent rather than actual articles, in the sense that when the dog finds the scent there is no physical item right there with it, the use of secondary finds are useful. When the dog hits the scent you can acknowledge it, praise the dog and work on. You can quickly place a find (secondary find) behind you, at the scent. Or you can work on to a find an article/s further on in the search. To place a find at the hide, drop it out of your left back pocket using your left hand, while you guide your dog around to the right using your right hand in order to work up to the hide again, this time with an article for your dog to retrieve. This is not always easy, so an assistant is an asset. Of course, at this stage your dog should be able to work one or two searches with no reward except some praise from you. Very challenging. And very realistic.

Be creative, think about how people smuggle things and use their items to conceal stuff and you will find a whole world of ingenious hides.

Indoor Advanced Searches

You can hide scented labels, such as small or cut up Post-it® notes, or tiny articles like half a scented cotton bud that the dog will not get to retrieve in the cracks around cupboard or entrance doors, windows and behind pictures or signs. You can even smear some scent onto walls or floorboards. In these searches, you acknowledge the indication at the correct spot (hide) and either work the dog on with no further find or place a secondary find out for him right at the hide or somewhere else in the search area.

Make the search area either very barren or very busy. Both will provide a challenge. Litter the area with whatever you think will distract your dog. This could be toys, dogs or children, depending on your resources! Or the ultimate distraction for many dogs - food. Operational dogs have to search kitchens, galleys, post-flight passenger planes and domestic houses. So introducing food in containers or on tables, etc.

depending on how tempted your dog is, can make for a super challenging search area.

Baggage

Fill the cases or bags. You can work on all types of skills here. You can recreate hand baggage or luggage. Fill hand baggage with books, make up bags, pencil cases, etc. For practical purposes, don't put gadgets or phones inside they might get broken when dogs are working on active indications. On the other hand, if you have old stuff that won't harm the dog and you don't mind if they get broken, go for it. Think like a smuggler. With clothing, throwing it into the case will provide a good level of difficulty, rolling it will step it up, but folding it neatly and filling the case to the brim will be the most realistic and also the most difficult. The more layers the scent needs to work through, the trickier the search.

If you have access to hard shell suitcases, you can see just how well you've trained your dog. Allow him to walk over the case, and give it a squeeze yourself to force the air out of the zip closure or rubber seal in the middle of the case. Scent will travel out with the expelled air.

You can line the bags up close enough so they touch each other during the initial part of the search. As the search continues, move the bags around to give the dog more access to them. You can open the zips a little as your dog comes to each case. This lets him get the first whiff of scent as the air finds the opening and leaves the baggage.

Outdoor Advanced Searches

You can really vary the heights of the hides when working outdoors. Use fences, hedges, walls, equipment, machinery, bushes, trees, whatever the location offers. Don't overlook 'blank' areas. The classic one is grass. If you are working in grassed or slate/stone covered areas, the hide could be in the middle. Often handlers concentrate on working the perimeters when outside, but the middle can be just as challenging. Hide it under the stones or amongst the grass. You can even bury the articles, not feet deep but certainly under the surface. These searches are really fun.

Postal

Adding more post to the sacks, and carefully choosing what type of post will instantly increase the challenge of postal searches. Try lifting a full postal sack and you will find it surprisingly heavy. The weight of the post compresses the scent, the density of the contents make it difficult for the air, and therefore the scent, to circulate around the items inside the bags. The more plastic, as in padded bags, or glossy paper, as in junk mail, that you add to the sack, the more difficult the search becomes.

Instead of lining the bags up, you can set them out in a big pile that the dog then has to rifle through. You will still be on hand to move the bags and assist in the search, but this simple change in presentation of the search items will add a twist to the search. This presentation is better done off lead.

Scent discrimination as a specific exercise

During each and every search your dog is constantly discriminating between scents, looking for the one he associates with his reward. Everything has it's own scent. Plus contamination from whatever it has come into contact with, be that your scent, the cat, the children, the smell of last's night's dinner, the plug in air freshener, and on, and on . . .

But at this stage in his scentwork career it's useful, and fun, to test your dog to ensure that you have taught him to search for the scent not the scented article. Hide unscented articles, unscented jars, articles with non-trained scents, in addition to the actual scent that your dog is trained to find. If the dog indicates on the wrong article, move him on and continue searching. If he consistently gives false indications, you need to go back a few steps and remind him of the scent you want him to find. Do this by scenting up a greater variety of articles so that he doesn't associate a particular article with the scent.

You can pare this down a little by using identical hides. Set up a row of 5 identical boxes / jars / containers. Put an unscented article in one hide and a scented article in another. Then work the line. Increase the number of scented and unscented articles as the dog continues to be successful. If he is unsuccessful, keep things simple and pare it back a bit.

You can then put out a scented article and an article with a distinct non-trained scent to see if the dog can discriminate between the two. Bear in mind that everything has a scent so the dog is discriminating between scents all the time during every single search. But by adding a particularly strong scent that you do not want to the dog to indicate on, you increase the challenge. Stronger scent = bigger scent picture = more chance that the dog will find it interesting. This is a good challenge for the handler too. You can see the dog smelling the new scent but can you see him indicating? Scenting and indicating are not the same things. You might smell a cake in the oven but you don't necessarily act on it by walking to the oven.

Note

Remember, some pet dogs without the high drive of professional working dogs, can flounder when the scent picture is reduced or when secondary aids are introduced. Find your dog's level.

Part 7

Troubleshooting

TROUBLESHOOTING

Dog picks up random, non-scented items

If the dog starts to pick up random objects during the search, this can mean that he is frustrated or over-excited. This dog needs calm support to resume searching properly and confidently rather than guessing which object you want him to retrieve. If possible, continue searching, ignoring the object your dog has picked up. As he begins to use his nose, he may spit the object out. After all, if you don't value it, it's of no use to him. Alternatively, you can take the object from him and then carry on searching, discretely giving it to an assistant or disposing of it outside the search area yourself. Do not scold the dog for picking it up, he is trying to find the scented article. If you scold him for making a mistake, he may lose confidence and the desire to continue searching.

Frustration can kick in if the search has gone on too long for the dog's level of experience. If this is the case, either place an additional find in the area for him to hit quickly, or conduct a more thorough search of the area around the find. If you do a more thorough search and even though the dog is on top of the hide he does not indicate, quickly put out another find for him. It may be that he isn't sure what he is looking for, the object has several competing scents on it or that the air flow around the find is causing confusion. But whatever the reason, note it down so that as confidence grows you can revisit the situation in order to work through it. Following incidents like this with a couple of simple, quick fire, known searches will allow the handler to restore the dog's confidence quickly and efficiently. They shouldn't lead the dog to the find, but they can make more pointed suggestions as to which areas are worthy of closer inspection or multiple scans.

This situation is a great example of when a good assistant can be invaluable. If they have placed the find for you, then they can direct you to specific areas if the dog is becoming frustrated or demoralized. They need not tell you where it is, but they can suggest that you search just the left of the area or only in the middle of the area. They can also have a second article ready to hide for you should the need arise, or take the random object from you and remove it from the search area.

I have also seen this behaviour when a dog hits the scent very quickly but the handler misses the indication. This can send the dog into a highly agitated and confused state. He doesn't know what he should be looking for because he was called away or ignored when he did hit the actual scent. This issue can be addressed by doing several, quick fire, known searches. The article should be easy for the dog to retrieve, e.g. just sitting in an open box or behind a table. This issue here does not lie with the dog. It lies with the handler. The handler must improve their observational skills and be very clear on what they are looking for. Videoing searches can be a great help with this.

The dog is confused and won't search the cardboard boxes

This generally happens when dogs have been taught an alternative behaviour involving boxes. I can always tell if a dog has been taught to step inside the box or put his paw on it or stand on it. I recall one Irish Setter who worked his way around the boxes in the search area, standing on each one, looking very pleased with himself when he did so. His owner confirmed that he's been taught to this and that he really enjoyed it. The answer? Remove all the boxes from the room. This dog searched chairs during the workshop. He worked beautifully and found every bit of cheese we hid for him. So, if previous training adds confusion remove the item, e.g. the cardboard box, and replace it with something more appropriate.

Some dogs are worried by the boxes and don't want to touch them or put their heads inside. This cautious behaviour can show that the dog is a little anxious or doesn't cope well in new situations. Talking Dogs Scentwork® can help build the dog's confidence by teaching that it's very worthwhile putting your head into a box if it will result in the dog finding the article. Build confidence by using completely open boxes at first. You can play games by tossing the article into multiple open boxes for the dog to fetch, or cheese for him to eat. Do this in full view of the dog. This process is about building confidence around unusual articles, not about scentworking. Building confidence in this way can generalize to other areas of the dog's life.

If you are asking too much of the dog and he remains worried about the boxes, or any other specific items, then the answer is simple – remove them from the area.

Dog works too fast

Speed in searching is only detrimental if the dog is going too fast to find the article. The handler must adjust their pace to match the dog. Working too slowly is likely to result in the dog ignoring you and leaving you behind. This does not mean that you need to sprint around the area. Instead, plan ahead and anticipate where the dog will go, moving quickly to the areas you want him to cover, not waiting for him to get there and then following him over – one of the most common handling errors I see. Some dogs work very well at speed, appearing not to be working. But the test is that when they go over the hide they catch the scent and work it thoroughly. If your dog does this, then his pace is fine. However, if the dog is not actually scenting efficiently, it will take longer to locate the hide. This can cause frustration in the dog and can leave the handler unsure about the dog's search skills. I have found that the best way to address this is to present the dog with more challenging search areas. Place more boxes and containers in the area, increase the size of the area and the variety of hide locations to include those both high and low. Put the article inside a couple of boxes to decrease the scent picture. Or use chairs and other objects to form a puzzle for dogs who rip up the boxes in their excitement to locate the article. The dog will quickly realise that he has to be more thorough in order to find the prize so most will naturally slow themselves down. By controlling the hide and the search area, you, the handler, give the dog the reason to slow down without impeding his progress and stifling his enthusiasm.

Some dogs need extra help in slowing and searching more thoroughly. On lead directed searches can really help them to focus on more specific areas rather than trying to tackle the whole area in one go.

Dog ignores the handler

Some dogs have learned to work without their handler's assistance. Others think they can do it on their own. Both types of dog need to be taught the relevance of the handler. The handler will help them find the article faster. The handler will suggest areas that they might not have searched. The handler might even suggest areas that have already been searched, and hey presto! There it is! Active participation in the search by the handler resulting in the dog finding the article in areas suggested by the handler will quickly alert the dog to the advantages of keeping an eye on where the handlers moves to and what they are doing.

If you find that despite you helping him find the article more quickly he still ignores you, consider how you are working. You are probably moving too slowly and are a beat behind the rhythm of the search. Up your pace, and try to lead the search more by using the search patterns. The search patterns help you to keep the search flowing. Too much starting and stopping while you decide where to go next will result in the dog moving on and leaving you behind.

Dog is lack luster or ignores the article

Some dogs can appear not to enjoy the search. While others enjoy the search so much that when they find the article they almost ignore it and carry on searching, the search itself being more rewarding than the actual find. This typifies the response that can be the result of the dog not loving the result of finding the article. The easiest fix is to increase the excitement, duration and fun of the game or change the reward that comes after the click. But often it is the scented item or chosen food itself that, rather than being a great reward for searching, is actually a disincentive to the dog working. Consider how you'd feel at the end of the month if you received a certificate commending you for all your hard work. Wouldn't you feel short changed? Cheated? The dog can feel the same sense of being cheated if, at the end of the search he finds a catnip scented mouse when he doesn't really like to play. You would prefer to receive cash. He might prefer to receive cheese. There is little point in plodding on working a half hearted dog so that he finds catnip when if you simply changed to a food find he's become genuinely enthusiastic and happy to look for more. I know there are people who do not believe that teaching the dog to find food is as valid, impressive or skilled as finding a non-food scent. To put it bluntly, this is nonsense. Both have their own distinctive scent. The dog finds them by successfully identifying the scent. The only difference is that when they find the non-food scent they play or retrieve the article, and when they find the food article they eat it. To deny the dog the article he actually wants to find in favour of one the handler would prefer is to take the fun out of scentwork. You can build more drive for the non-food article, especially if your dog already likes to play but could do with being a bit more enthusiastic about the game. You can click and treat for any attention to the article, building up to a solid search and retrieve. The true strength of this learned behaviour will become apparent as the searches become more challenging. It has to be super strong to drive the dog forward to search for it over long periods or dig it out from tough hides. Personally, I would rather allow the dog to search for something he naturally values, give the dog what he wants.

Dog doesn't pick up the article

Go back to basics and work on the retrieve exercise to solve this one. This is how I teach the retrieve:

1. Find a toy that is easy for your dog to pick up and carry.

2. Begin by getting your dog to play with the toy. Have a really exuberant, exciting game with him. You can gee the dog up by teasing him with toy, snatching it away before he gets to it and wiggling it along the ground. Pushing the toy directly at

the dog or towards his mouth does not usually encourage him to play, but moving the toy like a small prey animal does.

3. Next, throw the toy a short distance, encouraging your dog to chase and pick up the toy. Run alongside the dog as if in competition to get the toy. If your dog does not pick the toy up when he reaches it, quickly grab the toy and throw it again. If your dog thinks that you want the toy he will be more motivated to try and grab it first. Once your dog has the toy do not try to touch or take the toy away from him, you want him to hang on to it and enjoy playing with it. The 'drop' will come later.

4. Run backwards in an excited and encouraging way so that he follows you while carrying the toy. If he doesn't want to come back to you, help him by clapping your hands, dropping down to one knee and opening your arms to make a welcoming target. If he comes back reward this with a big fuss or a titbit, still not touching the toy.

5. Once your dog is reliably bringing the toy back to you, introduce the word 'Fetch' so that he associates the word 'Fetch' with the action of running out to pick up the toy.

6. The next step is to ask him to drop the toy, either into your hand or onto the ground. If he's still unsure about this, revise the drop routine (see below.)

7. If you have been working on steps 1-6 on lead, you are now ready to repeat those steps off lead. This means that you can run towards the toy

without the danger of stopping him with the lead, i.e. if he runs faster than you!

8. Next, off lead, throw the toy a short distance and encourage your dog to 'Fetch' and pick the toy up. Start to run alongside the dog as if in competition to get the toy, but rather than running all the way to the toy, hang back as your dog passes you so that he reaches it while you are a little way off. Then when he picks it up you can run backwards encouraging him to return to you with the toy. Gradually reduce the distance you run towards the toy so that you end up standing still while your dog chases the toy.

Dog will not let go of the article or bring it to you

Go back to basics and work on the drop exercise to solve this one. This is how I teach the drop:

1. When playing with a toy, offer a titbit to your dog by holding a treat at the end of his nose, so that he swaps the toy for the titbit. *Hint – make no attempt to touch the toy when he drops it*. If you are playing a tuggy game, keep hold of the toy, but stop pulling when you present the titbit. Keep the toy close to the dog as he eats the titbit so that he can immediately resume the game. If, when your dog drops the toy, you immediately whip it away he will be less likely to drop it next time. By leaving the toy beside the dog, he gets the titbit and the toy, a win-win proposition that he'd be mad to turn down.

2. Once your dog is reliably dropping the toy the instant he sees the titbit, you can insert the

verbal cue, e.g. 'Drop'. Say 'Drop', then produce the titbit as before and swap it for the toy.

3. Now try saying 'Drop' and only producing the titbit once the dog has dropped the toy.

4. As the 'Drop' becomes more reliable, phase out the titbit altogether, with the reward for him dropping the toy simply being getting it back!

Practise the 'Drop' with a variety of toys. If your dog needs some help, try working with a less exciting toy or a tastier treat. Your dog is more likely to hang on to his favourite toy than his least favourite. Also, at the start, always return the toy to him. This will prevent him from thinking that dropping the item will automatically mean he's going to lose it. This is important as in an emergency situation you need him to let go of whatever he's found immediately, usually with the expectation of a reward. If you've not practised 'Drop' he may worry that you will scold him, take his 'treasure' away or both in which case he could guard the item. Never trick the dog, never snatch for the toy, always give the treats freely, sometimes dropping the treats on the floor, letting the dog drop the toy, eat the treats then pick the toy back up again. Next time drop the treats and the dog will be more likely to drop the toy, safe in the knowledge that you are not going to snatch it away from him. Drop more treats in a line away from the toy until you can calmly pick up the toy without any competition from the dog.

Once you have a reliable drop for the food reward, you can use this at the end of your searches. When the dog finds the article and brings it to you, he can be rewarded with a food treat.

Glossary

Hide – place where the article is hidden

Article (aka find) – the scented object you want your dog to find

Secondary article/find – a find put out as a reward for completing a blank search

Throw-in – the process of introducing the dog to a new scent

Active (aka proactive) – the dog retrieves / makes contact with the find

Passive – dog indicates by coming to a stop, can be a sit, down or stand, at the hide. Dog does not come into contact with the find.

Drive in – verbal commentary to help maintain the dog's drive to locate the find precisely

Free search – when the dog searches with minimal obvious guidance from the handler

Directed search – a thorough, systematic, detailed search

Blind search – when the handler does not know the location of the hide

Known search – when the handler knows the location of the hide

Blank search – when there is no pre-placed find/article

Scent picture – the plume or movement of scent that the dog detects

Scent / vapour trail – when scent lingers in the air allowing the dog to follow it to source

Resources

The home of Talking Dogs Scentwork® -
www.scentwork.com

Catac working dog harness – www.catac.co.uk

Karenswood, working dog equipment –
www.karenswood.co.uk

References

How scent and Airflow works
http://houndandthefound.wordpress.com/2012/02/22/how-scent-and-airflow-works/

The Kinetic Theory of Gases
http://chemwiki.ucdavis.edu/Physical_Chemistry/Physical_Properties_of_Matter/Gases/Kinetic_Theory_of_Gases

Abrantes, Roger, PhD, *The Mathematician Rat – An Evolutionary Explanation*
http://rogerabrantes.wordpress.com/2012/09/03/the-mathematician-rat-an-evolutionary-explanation/

Kjell B., Doving and Didier Trotier, *Structure and function of the vomeronasal organ*, The Journal of Experimental Biology 201, 2913-2925 (1998)

White, Steve, *i2i K9 Division of Labor*,
http://www.i2ik9.com/division%20of%20labor.htm

Kvam, Anne Lill, *Scent Discrimination: advanced technique made simple*
http://www.k9magazinefree.com/k9_perspective/iss20p6.shtml

Helton, William, S. (Ed), *Canine Ergonomics: The Science of Working Dogs*, 2009, CRC Press

Kidd, Randy, DVM, PhD *The Canine Sense of Smell* The Whole Dog Journal, Nov 2004

Tess Thompson *How the canine respiratory system works*
http://www.nativeremedies.com/petalive/articles/canine-respiratory-system.html

What does space smell like?
http://www.educatinghumanity.com/2012/08/Space-Smells-NASA-is-Reproducing-the-Odor.html

What does space smell like?
http://www.inquisitr.com/287901/what-does-space-smell-like-nasa-astronauts-explain-the-stench/